OXFORD

1   Magdalen Tower

From Ackermann's
" History of the University
of Oxford" (1814)

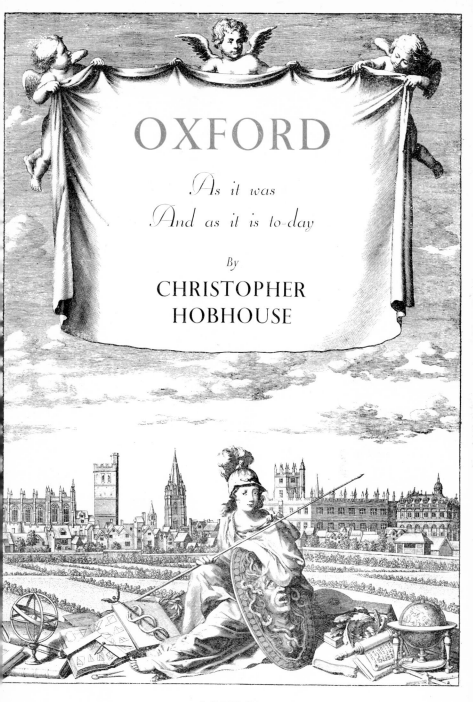

OXFORD

As it was
And as it is to-day

By

CHRISTOPHER
HOBHOUSE

LONDON

B. T. BATSFORD LTD., 15 NORTH AUDLEY STREET, W.1

And WALTON VILLA, MALVERN WELLS, WORCS.

First published, September 1939
Second printing, Winter 1941–2

MADE AND PRINTED IN GREAT BRITAIN
BY WILLIAM CLOWES AND SONS, LIMITED
LONDON AND BECCLES

TO DENISE

NOTE TO SECOND EDITION

CHRISTOPHER HOBHOUSE, who joined the Fighting Services soon after the publication of this book, was killed on active service in England early in 1940. His premature death not only cut short a brilliant career, but was a major literary loss of the war.

The early call for a second edition has provided the opportunity to incorporate such slight corrections as reviewers and correspondents have pointed out, and to replace one or two illustrations; otherwise the book is re-issued in its original form.

THE PUBLISHERS.

ACKNOWLEDGMENT

THE Publishers are particularly indebted to Mr. A. F. Kersting, F.R.P.S., and Mr. L. A. Audrain, who took specially the majority of the photographs which illustrate this book : Mr. Kersting those on Figs. 4, 5, 8, 9, 13, 15, 17, 23, 25, 26, 37, 39, 51, 53, 54, 55, 64, 67, 68, 71, 72, 73, 75, 76, 77, 78, 79, 83, 86, 87, 101, 102, 104, 106, 134 and 135 ; and Mr. Audrain those on Figs. 2, 19, 29, 66, 82, 107, 110, 113, 114, 115, 116, 117, 118, 123, 125, 126, 129, 130 and 131. They must also thank Messrs. Aerofilms, Ltd., for Figs. 112 and 128 ; Mr. J. Dixon-Scott, F.R.P.S., for Figs. 7, 24 and 105 ; Messrs. F. Frith & Co., Ltd., Reigate, 27 ; Messrs. Dorien Leigh, Ltd., for Figs. 84 and 120 ; Mr. Herbert Felton, F.R.P.S., for Figs. 6, 34 and 65 ; Messrs. Fox Photos, Ltd., for Figs. 108, 109, 111, 119, 132 and 133 ; Messrs. General Photographic Agency, Ltd., for Fig. 89 ; Mr. Lucien Myers, for Fig. 11 ; the Librarian of the Oxford City Library, for Figs. 88, 99 and 100 ; Mr. John H. Stone, for Figs. 21, 27, 127 and 138 ; Mr. Will F. Taylor, for Figs. 10, 28, 46, 74, 80, 81, 85, 103, 124, 136 and 137 ; and the Oxford Union Society, for Figs. 121 and 122. The remaining subjects have been taken for the most part from originals in the Publishers' Collection. The back endpaper of a Map of Oxford in 1675 has been reproduced from David Loggan's *Oxonia Illustrata*, while the front endpaper was specially drawn by Miss Norah Davenport.

CONTENTS

x

2 *(opposite)* : On the Towpath

Mediæval Oxford
as it was

FRIDESWIDE, THE DAUGHTER OF "KING" DIDAN, BEING pursued by an importunate though royal lover, had taken refuge in a pigsty, when she was relieved to learn that her tormentor had miraculously been struck with blindness. She celebrated the removal of this menace to her chastity by the foundation of a priory, close to a spit of gravel where oxen were wont to ford the Thames. This was about the year 700, and it is the first we know about Oxford, mythology apart. The place was never a Roman settlement. The actual name of Oxford first occurs in the *Anglo-Saxon Chronicle* for the year 912, when it is referred to as though it were a place of some importance. And it has been suggested that about this time the tall mound which can be seen in the grounds of the prison on the way from the railway station was erected as a protection against the Danes.[1]

Oxford was clearly cut out for a place of importance. It stood on the boundaries of Mercia and Wessex ; it was protected by the Thames on two sides and on a third by the Cherwell ; to a primitive strategist the two rivers form a peninsula of some integrity. It was taken and burnt by Danes in 1010 ; in 1018 the great Canute, as King of Denmark and all England, held a *gemot* in Oxford, where he made fine promises to rule justly ; and at Oxford his son Harold was crowned. Thus before the Norman Conquest Oxford already served as an occasional capital city. But shortly after, whether through pestilence or fire or through the severity of the conqueror, the town suffered some mysterious disaster. No man knows the cause of it : but Domesday Book records that Oxford has rather more than a thousand houses of which the half are in ruins, together with eight churches and two thousand inhabitants. The Norman governor of this stricken town was a Robert d'Oily,

---

[1] This mound is now thought to have been proved to be of Norman origin ; but it has been argued that it is clearly set up as a defence against attack from the river, which was the Danish method of approach.

2   1

3 (*opposite*) : Tom Tower from St. Aldate's Churchyard (*Ackermann's " Oxford"*)

who not only left behind him the great square tower of the Castle
at the western end of the town, but also either built or repaired
the tower of St. Michael's beside the north gate, that curious
rough rubble tower at the top of the Cornmarket. West of the
town d'Oily's nephew and successor founded an immense priory,
later the Abbey of Osney, of which only a doorway now remains,
not far from the Great Western Railway station. The Castle stood
by the road which led to Osney and the West Country; St.
Michael's stood by the road which led north to royal Woodstock:
and the two roads crossed at the Carrefours, or Quatrevois or
Carfax, then as now. The tower at Carfax is the tower of St.
Martin's Church, which stood there a full thirty years before the
Norman Conquest. To the north-west of Carfax, where Beaumont
Street now runs, Henry I built Beaumont Palace, of which there
is no trace remaining. His daughter Matilda took refuge in the
Castle from her cousin Stephen; but being closely besieged for
several weeks, she slipped out one night across the frozen river and
got away to Abingdon. Henry II favoured the people of Oxford
with a charter in the year 1155; and two years later his son
Richard Cœur de Lion was born in Beaumont Palace.

What schools or teachers there may have been in Oxford during
the hundred years that followed the Norman Conquest nobody
knows. At that time any Englishman in search of learning would
have most likely made his way to the great University of Paris.
But in the year 1167 there was a migration from Paris to Oxford.
Some say that Henry II recalled the English students; some say
that the French expelled them. Be that as it may, it is improbable
that they would have chosen to come to Oxford if the town had not
already been known for its teaching. But it is from that date
onwards that Oxford became known and recognised as a place of
general resort for men of learning.

The town to which these scholars of Paris transferred was not
yet encircled with the massive wall whose remnants still bind it
together. These fortifications were probably built in the next
century. In 1167 most of the houses were of wood, and those
which were built of stone belonged for the most part to the Jews,
who abounded in the town. There existed a great hatred between
the Jewry and the Priory of St. Frideswide; while what with St.
Frideswide's and Osney Abbey, the mercenary citizens had quite
enough of piety and learning. So the poor students, unprivileged
and unendowed, were hard put to it to get a foothold in the place.
A later ordinance by which the Jews were forbidden to charge
them interest at more than 43 per cent. gives some idea of the sort
of difficulty with which their slender means contended.

To circumvent the hostility of the citizens and the extortion
of the landlords, the scholars were forced to band themselves
together. Instead of lodging out in all manner of houses and inns,

4 Part of the City Wall in New College Garden

5 The Lodge, New College

6   Merton College Chapel

as they had done (and as their successors still do) in Paris, they began to lodge in "halls" of their own, rented or bought by a co-operative effort, and each ruled by a principal elected among its members. In these halls they lived and dined ; but for their instruction they went out to any teacher in the town, for every teacher, good or bad, was at liberty to set up his own school on whatever terms he pleased.

Within fifty years of the first influx of students this defenceless community was all but extinguished for good. In the year 1209 a scholar while practising his archery killed a good woman in the street. There ensued a terrible row. The city, longing to be rid of the whole pack of penniless clerks, took reprisal by hanging a few of them with the connivance of the bad King John. The remainder fled from the town, some of them to a still less healthy spot in the fenlands, where they started the University of Cambridge.

For five years the infant university remained suspended, until a Papal Legate reinstated it, conferring many privileges upon the scholars and corresponding penances upon the town. From this time onwards the university was a cuckoo in the nest so far as the city was concerned. The townsmen were no longer able to arrest a scholar ; instead they must hand him over to an official called the Chancellor. Shortly after other officials called proctors made their appearance, whose business was to maintain a separate discipline among the scholars. In spite of these measures, town and gown often came to blows ; but the outcome of every conflict was a fresh humiliation of the city and a fresh set of privileges for the university, whose interests were kindly regarded by the powers of Church and State.

Yet in spite of the protection of the great, the university was so desperately poor that many of its scholars were barely kept from starvation. Their community would scarcely have survived if it had not been for the arrival of the friars, whose influence was dominant throughout the thirteenth century. In 1221 the first Dominicans came from Bologna to Oxford and set to work to convert the Oxford Jews, with marvellous success. In 1224 the first Franciscans followed, and began their work of helping the poor, the sick, and the leprous. These bodies were followed by the Carmelites and later the Augustinians, who set up a friary where Wadham College now stands.

The friars made Oxford its reputation. Their good works and their excellent teaching put the whole breed of monks to shame. Until they had arrived the leading figure in Oxford's history had been Edmund Rich, who had taught divinity and canon law in a house where St. Edmund Hall now consecrates his memory. He is Oxford's first saint ; but after he had left to become Archbishop of Canterbury, there began a period of great leaders and teachers.

The leading figure of this period is Robert Grosseteste. He was not a friar himself—indeed, he was a rather worldly ecclesiastic—but he acted as the first rector to the newly arrived Franciscans and one of the first Chancellors of the university.[1] Roger Bacon was probably a pupil of both Rich and Grosseteste. He was a Franciscan, though his brethren mistrusted his inquiring mind. From Oxford he went on, as many students did, to Paris ; and from Paris he returned to his famous study on Folly Bridge, where for many years he groped his way through the darkness of his times, catching faint glimmers of reflected light where no other man had seen a thing. From grammar to astrology, from logic to alchemy, he pursued his searches into every corner of knowledge, collecting fragments of wisdom and fragments of trash into one amazing brain.

Paris at this epoch still stood easily supreme among universities. Paris also had its town-and-gown disturbances, and in 1229, after a riot of exceptional severity, there was a fresh exodus of English students from thence to Oxford. One of these was a certain William who later became Archdeacon of Durham, and died in 1249, leaving to the hospitable university a sum of 310 marks [2] for the endowment of masters of arts. This legacy was an astonishment to the university, whose staple income hitherto had been a shilling a week paid as a fine for the misbehaviour of the townsmen in 1209. This weekly shilling was paid by Grosseteste into a university " chest " from which loans were made to the poorest scholars. But three hundred marks was a very different matter, and since the most urgent need was to strengthen the segregation of the " halls " from the city, the authorities used the money in the purchase of what is now University College.

This is therefore the first college to acquire a habitation, though it did not attain its own statutes until the year 1280, and it may be argued that the possession of a body of statutes is the distinguishing feature of a college. If that is so, then University College cannot claim an absolute priority ; for things were moving fast, and the example of William of Durham was swiftly followed by others. The Bishop of Durham, edified by the generosity of his late archdeacon, decided to achieve a similar end at someone else's expense. So when in 1260 John de Balliol, one of the regents of Scotland, made himself unduly odious to the episcopal authorities, the Bishop not only flogged him at his own cathedral door, but also commanded him by way of penance to endow a hostel for sixteen students at Oxford. Balliol can therefore claim to be the second college to be endowed and settled on its present site,

---

[1] Another Oxford saint of the thirteenth century was Thomas Cantelupe, a great pluralist and politician, lawyer and theologian, who twice became Chancellor of the university in the course of his very active career.

[2] About £2000 of our money.

though Sir John's designs were not carried through until after his death, when his energetic widow Dervorguilla came to Oxford for the purpose.

But while both University and Balliol were waiting for their statutes, one Walter de Merton had stolen a march on both. He was Lord Chancellor to Henry III, so that money and manors came to his bidding. His first idea, formed in about 1263, had been to found a college at his country place in Surrey; but he soon transferred to Oxford, and by 1274 he had not only bought his site and begun his buildings, but had secured a charter and statutes as well. Merton College therefore asserts itself to be the first of colleges, and there is one good reason why the claim should be supported, for it is the only one of these first three which has retained its founder's buildings.

Walter de Merton was a former student of Oxford who had risen to be Bishop of Rochester. It is significant that he laid down that any member of his college should be compelled to leave if he should take monastic vows. But though he aimed at a secular house, he was to give it a magnificent chapel, in which the uses of an oratory and a parish church were to be combined. Merton Chapel, of which only the half was ever built, was planned on the scale of a cathedral. For the next hundred and fifty years it arose by stages : the windows of its choir glowed in the faint lights of the thirteenth century ; its tower was raised in time to catch the first glimmer of the Renaissance.

It is time to leave the thirteenth century. At its opening, a few poor scholars had been struggling to exist among a hostile crowd of merchants. Before it closed, a community of some thousands were building themselves three great colleges, with libraries, halls, and sumptuous places of worship. No longer was the university huddled into a little triangle around Carfax and St. Mary's Church. Merton was built to the south, abutting on the new city walls. Balliol, by a still bolder stroke, was laid outside the north gate, well beyond the wide ditch, so as not to impede the flight of arrows. Alongside of Balliol on the same side of Canditch arose the new Durham Hall, endowed by two Bishops of Durham for the use of Benedictines. To the east, where Wadham stands, was the new Augustinian friary. And a long way to the west, set away by Beaumont Palace, to be at a distance from the distractions of the town, was a little cluster of houses each maintained by a separate diocese for the use of its own Benedictine scholars, and known collectively as Gloucester Hall. Every one of these new centres of piety and learning was a product of the years from 1260 to 1300 ; while the miraculous tower and spire of St. Mary's, the university church, were raised at the turn of the century between 1290 and 1310.

The fourteenth century added four more colleges to the list.

A Bishop of Exeter founded Exeter College for the students of the West Country. Oriel College was founded twice over, once by Adam de Brome, the rector of St. Mary's and almoner to King Edward II, and again two years later by the King himself. The Queen's College was founded by one Robert Eglesfield, chaplain to Queen Philippa, for the benefit of students from Cumberland and Westmorland. In this same period a certain Bishop Cobham also added to the old fabric of St. Mary's the curious crypt known as the Old Congregation House, where the authorities of the university thereafter met and deliberated, dealt out justice, hoarded treasure, and brought together their first diminutive collection of books.

All these benefactors were in holy orders ; and, indeed, the greater part of Oxford has been built at the expense of clerics. This was due to two things that the Reformation killed—celibacy and pluralism. A successful cleric of the Middle Ages might accumulate any number of benefices and enjoy their large and elastic revenues ; but if he kept his vows, he would have no heirs to inherit his savings. Sometimes he bethought himself of the cold, comfortless halls where he had learnt his divinity, of the days when there was no food to be had, of the friends with whom he used to stamp in unison up and down the fireless rooms. And he would decide that his own hall should have his endowment for the future, and should extend to its pupils the shelter and security of a college. From such impulses came the wealth of Oxford.

Exeter, Oriel, and Queen's have all discarded their original buildings for newer and grander edifices. No doubt their beginnings were small, but so was Oxford itself ; and the erection within a narrow walled city of so many new and costly works gave to the citizens a cause for much misgiving and jealousy. Their ancient grievances, by no means soothed by two hundred years of proximity, came to a head in the classic " town and gown " riot of 1354. On February 10th of that year, the feast of St. Scholastica the Virgin, a number of scholars looked in for a drink at a tavern aptly named Swyndlestock. " There calling for wine, John de Croydon the vintner brought them some, but they disliking it, as it should seem, and he avouching it to be good, several snappish words passed between them. At length the vintner giving them stubborn and saucy language, they threw the wine and vessel at his head. The vintner therefore receding with great passion, and aggravating the abuse to those of his family and neighbourhood, several came in, encouraged him not to put up the abuse, and withal told him they would faithfully stand by him." Other citizens " out of propensed malice seeking all occasions of conflict with the Scholars " took up the vintner's cause, and caused the bell of St. Martin's in Carfax Tower to be rung. This was always a tocsin to the townsmen in their clashes with the gown. The Chancellor came forward to appease the tumult, but was shot at

7, 8   New College : two views of the Front Quad

9   New College : the Tower and Cloister

with bows and arrows ; retreating, he " caused the University Bell at St. Mary's to be rung out, whereupon the scholars got bows and arrows and maintained the fight with the townsmen till dark night." Next day the townsmen enlisted the help of the country-folk around Oxford ; the two bells were rung again ; many of the scholars were killed and five of their halls broke open with fire and sword. In the evening there arrived a proclamation in the King's name, but the townsmen paid no heed to it. More of the halls were looted ; Merton College, to which most of the scholars retreated as a stronghold, was besieged for a week ; and some sixty-three scholars in all were killed, so that " the gutter of Brewer's Lane ran with academic blood."

This outrage was severely visited upon the city. Apart from other reparations and safeguards, a penance was instituted, and on February 10th every year from 1355 until 1825 the mayor of Oxford and another sixty-two of the freemen were constrained to attend a service at St. Mary's and to offer a tribute of sixty-three pence. By such and other like measures did the university attain its exorbitant privileges over the inhospitable town.

Oxford had now definitely passed its two hundredth year, and its place in the national life was well assured. No less a man than Wyclif was Master of Balliol ; and Oxford men were gaining fame in every diocese and in every branch of the King's service. But the outstanding figure of the second half of the century was not an Oxford man at all. The fifty years prior to St. Scholastica's day had seen the foundation of three colleges. The next fifty years saw but one, and that the foundation of a man of very humble birth. William of Wykeham had risen to fame through the profession of architecture, and had become surveyor of the royal castles. In this capacity he manifested such uncommon talents that he was made Keeper of the Privy Seal at the age of forty, and four years later Chancellor. Moreover, having been ordained a priest at the height of his career, he was rapidly promoted to the great Bishopric of Winchester. There he devoted some of his great revenues to the foundation of his school at Winchester and of his college at Oxford for the supply not of monks but of " fit persons for the service of God in Church and State "—in other words, to give to others the advantages that he had lacked.

New College dates from 1379. In those days it was new in many aspects ; it was new in the scale of its endowments, in the admirable system of its statutes, new in its self-contained tutorial system, and newest of all in its plan and layout, every detail of which was contrived by Wykeham himself. New College is the work of a superb architect, and by good fortune its fabric has survived, little different from what it was when the Warden and scholars walked in tuneful procession to their new quarters five hundred and fifty years ago.

New College reached completion with the consecration of its cloisters in the year 1400. A new century opens, and the Middle Ages are drawing to an end. But before the burden of the Hundred Years War shall have been lifted from England, and the way left open to a rebirth of the humanities, there are two more foundations to be added to the seven that exist. In 1427, twelve years after Agincourt, we have the foundation of Lincoln College. Ten years later the war was still in progress when Henry Chichele, Archbishop of Canterbury, who had been one of the scholars who entered New College the day that it was opened, established his foundation of All Souls as a memorial and an offering (in the words of the royal warrant) " for the souls of the most illustrious Prince Henry, late King of England, of Thomas late Duke of Clarence our uncle, of the Dukes, Earls, Barons, Knights, Esquires, and other noble subjects of our father and ourselves who fell in the wars for the Crown of France, as also for the souls of all the faithful departed."

Upon this flourish of outspoken piety we take our leave of the Middle Ages.

10   Merton : the
     Library

11   Mediæval Roofs at Merton

Mediæval Oxford
as it is

IT IS TOLD OF PROFESSOR FREEMAN THAT WHEN AN AMERICAN
friend asked to be shown the oldest historical monument in
Oxford, he escorted the visitor to Port Meadow, a dank waste
on the outskirts of the town. This is a pasture held in common by
the freemen of Oxford ; it was so held in common at the time of
Domesday, which also records that it brought in 6s. 8d. yearly ;
and if one went back another nine hundred years before Domesday,
in all probability Port Meadow was held in common then.

Some limits must be placed upon the search for antiquities. In
the cathedral, for example, there are fragments of the original
chapel of St. Frideswide, burnt down with a party of Danes inside
it in the year 1001 ; but they are not worth a pilgrimage. The
Saxon mound is a noticeable object on the way to or from the railway station ; but one could build as good a mound or better in
one's own garden. The Castle Tower, less conspicuous, is a pure
Norman edifice ; but few people will go to the length of troubling
the Prison Governor for leave to examine its depressing precincts.

In search of real antiquity you need go no farther than the Cornmarket, the central shopping street of Oxford and one of the ugliest
streets in England. At its north end, beside where used to stand
the north gate, is the tower of St. Michael's Church, associated with
the name of Robert d'Oily. Its rough, thick walls, the round-
headed windows, narrow and defensive, the stout balusters which
divide them, all suggest a Saxon work, perhaps repaired by the
lavish Norman. The body of the church is nothing like as old, and
has suffered at the hands of George Edmund Street.

Walking south down the Cornmarket between a double file of
commercial eyesores, you come to Carfax, the very heart of Oxford.
The two southern corners of this crossing have lately been set back
and rebuilt in chaste symmetry. How narrow it once was can be
estimated by realising that the present tower is that of St. Martin's,
whose chancel projected into the road and was quite recently
removed. The tower is not that which Canute observed on his

3   9

Oxford visit, but a successor. It is, however, probably the same tower from whose belfry the town was called to arms on St. Scholastica's Day, and whose battlements were lowered on account of the mean practice of the townsmen in pelting the scholars with stones.

Southwards of Carfax towards Folly Bridge, where the oxen forded the Thames, runs the broad street called St. Aldate's : and though there is even a St. Aldate's Church on the right, it is a curious fact that no saint of any such name existed, while the name of neither street nor church is ever pronounced by any Oxonian as anything but " St. Old's." The truth of the matter is that the Old Gate spanned this road, and because Englishmen then spoke with what is now called an American accent, the name became corrupted, as did that of Aldgate in London. But it was characteristic of Oxford to canonise its own back door.

A hundred yards down this lovely slope, under Tom Tower and on the far side of Tom Quad, you see the spire of the cathedral, one of the oldest spires in England. The cathedral entrance is an inconspicuous double arch in the east wall of the vast quadrangle. This cathedral was originally part of the priory of St. Frideswide. As cathedrals go, it was never very large ; and Cardinal Wolsey made it smaller still by lopping off three bays to the west in order to have Tom Quad as large as he intended. The building had been finished, apart from its spire, in the year 1180 ; but it was started before the arrival of the scholars from Paris. The eastern half was begun first, and is typical round-arched Romanesque work ; the nave was finished several years later, by which time the influence of the Early English builders had been felt. The transition is subtly shown in the lighter and more elaborate piers and the pointed arches above them. Unfortunately all the piers have split capitals, springing arches of different heights, a form of architectural cheating which is extremely unpleasing to the eye and mind. The much purer Romanesque of the east wall, with its wheel window above, its arcade of interlaced arches, and two great round-headed windows below, is a product of the bold imagination of Sir George Gilbert Scott, and was introduced in 1871. But the splendid feature of the building is the choir roof, a stone-vaulted roof of the sixteenth century, admirable in effect and unique in the manner in which square vaults have been attained by thrusting the whole structure forward from the walls upon a row of pendants, from which the traceried fans are made to radiate.

Already this account is straying from the confines of the Middle Ages. The cathedral abounds in Civil War monuments and Victorian windows, which need no guide. It is time to visit the first of the colleges—Merton, which lies to the east of the cathedral on the straight line of the city wall.

Because it is the first of colleges, Merton is also the most untidy.

It awaited the genius of Wykeham to contrive the neat collegiate plan, and Merton in particular is laid out anyhow. From Merton Street you enter by a gateway which, together with the whole street front, was sadly knocked about by an early Victorian architect named Blore ; while in the hall, which faces you, you confront once again the staggering self-confidence of Gilbert Scott. However, in his rebuilding Scott did retain the massive basement and flight of stairs which distinguish this as the first communal building in Oxford ; and there is some remarkable original iron-work on the great oak door. Passing under a small arch to the right of the hall, you find a strange box-like building with a steep, smooth stone roof. This is the Treasury, built strong and fireproof to protect the college exchequer against just such contingencies as that of St. Scholastica's Day. Beyond the Treasury is the first of Oxford quadrangles, known to all generations for some unknown reason as Mob Quad. A spot more tranquil both to the ear and eye it would be hard to find. On the first floor, the south and west sides of this quadrangle comprise the library, whose tiny lancet windows date from the 1370's. The big comfortable dormers in the roof above were added in the Jacobean age, after eight genera-tions of readers had complained about the lighting. It is worth penetrating into this library if possible, for it is the oldest in Oxford and its cramped and studious atmosphere is impressive. Originally all the books were chained to the shelves.

Over the north-west angle of Mob Quad towers the chapel, whose choir was built about 1294. The style of that epoch was the Decorated, in which lancet windows began to be grouped into multiples to form a larger, composite window of variable size. The cold, greyish glass in the side windows is equally old ; not so the east window. Originally the chapel was intended to be immense, with a nave to counterbalance the choir ; but the building made slow progress. The antechapel, which in this instance should more correctly be called " the transepts," was not built till over a century later, by which time the Perpendicular style was dominant. Finally the noble Perpendicular tower was added in 1450–1. Then the nave was dropped. For one thing, it was not wanted. Secondly, by this time, as will be explained elsewhere, William of Wykeham had contrived the regular T-shaped plan for a college chapel, to which the existing building conformed. Thirdly, the founders of Corpus made an offer for the site. But to this day the rough stone on the west wall shows where the opening of the nave was meant to be.

At the south-east corner, outside the chapel and formerly con-nected with it by a squint, is the vestry, which the Victorians used as a brewhouse. Returning to the front quad, if quad it can be called, you find beyond the hall a very wide archway with a fine elaborate vault, built about 1500 and ornamented with the arms

of Henry VII and the signs of the zodiac. Through here is the
Fellows' Quad, a prim affair only notable for its rather tiresome
Jacobean sham tower, showing the various " orders " of architecture. The great room over the arch itself is called the Queen's
Room because it was occupied by Queen Henrietta Maria during
the Civil Wars. Charles I was lodged in Christ Church, and she is
said to have had a private route from one college to the other contrived by passing through the vestry and chapel. The Warden of
Merton at this time was a Parliament's man, so Charles I removed
him and put in William Harvey, the discoverer of the circulation
of the blood. Charles II also deposited his queen at Merton more
than once ; and not only his queen, for Lady Castlemaine and the
beautiful Miss Stuart were given rooms in Fellows' Quad, where
the former gave birth to a future Duke of Northumberland. But
in spite of all these royal womenfolk, Merton remained funda-
mentally unsound in politics compared with other colleges.

A less historic atmosphere prevails among the remaining buildings of Merton. The farther quadrangle to the east stands on the
site of St. Alban's Hall, more commonly known as Stubbins, an
institution which maintained its honoured independence until
1882, when in accordance with the policy of that time its existence
was merged in that of its powerful neighbour and landlord. The
present St. Alban's Quad is easily recognisable as the work of
Basil Champneys. It commands a fine aspect of the gardens,
which were formerly a famous place of resort for courtiers and
courtesans, until in 1720 the fellows decided that their amenities
were so much abused that they should be closed ; and they have
remained closed ever since. The raised terrace along the side of
the garden is, of course, a portion of the city wall, beneath which
on the other side runs the ill-famed Dead Man's Walk. In front
of the buildings of Fellows' Quad the wall has been cut down and
replaced by a fine iron railing. The view from Merton Fields to
the south, which are accessible by a passage between Merton and
Corpus, is certainly the most attractive view of Merton, embracing
all the harmonious lines of the two older portions. There is an
independent block of buildings in the foreground which was formerly one of the great eyesores of Oxford. It was built in 1864 by
Butterfield, who fancied his own style so much that he even proposed to demolish Mob Quad in order to extend the scope of his
improvements. Its pristine appearance can be judged by com-
parison with other works of Butterfield's which will later be
encountered. This specimen proved so offensive to a later generation that in 1930 it was refaced and otherwise civilised at great
expense and with much skill ; but it is still a thousand pities that
it should be there at all.

Apart from a modern residence for the warden, erected on the
other side of the road on the scale of a bishop's palace, that is all

13   New College Chapel

14   The Reynolds Window at New College (*Ackermann's " Oxford "*)

there is of Merton, one of the richest and most renowned of colleges. Making north by Grove Street, you come out into the High opposite to St. Mary's Church, the University Church which has figured so largely in the mediæval history of Oxford. The body of the church was rebuilt in the fifteenth century ; and the actual mediæval portions are the tower and spire and the additions on the northern side. From this side the great height and gigantic strength of the tower appear as an almost staggering testimony to the faith of the infant university of the year 1290. It must be acknowledged that the spire itself owes a good deal to later altera-tions, and hardly a stone of it can have heard the bells ring out that called the scholars to arms. In 1850 a Mr. Buckler raised the pinnacles ; but this measure added so dangerously to their weight that six years later Sir George Gilbert Scott had to make drastic alterations in the structure. A few years later the old statues were condemned and new ones substituted by Frampton. The original statues are now housed in the Old Congregation House, which should be entered by a door beside the foot of the tower.

This Congregation House, as has been said, was built in 1320 as a meeting-place for the heads of the university, and served that purpose for three centuries. Since then it has been put to every sort of odd use, and is strangely tenanted to-day. It is a bleak, depressing crypt, but full of memories. On the floor above it is a rather lovely room which served as the university library before the spacious days of Duke Humphrey. Now it is used as a parish room, in which earnest discussions are held upon the plight of Ethiopia and China. As for the church itself, it is so intimately linked with a later period of history that it would be well to include it in a later survey.

All Souls, lying beneath the shadow of St. Mary's spire, is some thirty years younger. New College, farther to the east, is a few years older. For history's sake let us first search the windings of New College Lane for its unobtrusive gateway. And in case the necessity arises of asking the way, it is well to know that New College, alone of all the colleges in Oxford, is invariably spoken of as " New College," and never in any circumstances as " New."

William of Wykeham embarked upon his great scheme with the most cut-and-dried conceptions both as to its architectural form and its educational method. His statutes are as admirable in their planning and forethought as his buildings. Over the entrance arch he provided a lodging for the warden, who could thus keep an eye upon the comings and goings of his students. In the days when boys went to Oxford at the age of eleven or twelve, this was a characteristically sound idea. Most later colleges copied it, and placed their head in an oriel above the gate ; but at later periods they have all abandoned this arrangement save New College.

The front quadrangle has undergone two great alterations since it was built. Sash windows have taken the place of mullions and an extra storey has been added. Otherwise the whole stands almost as it did in 1387, when the builders left. There is a curious feature in the fenestration, which is due to Wykeham's minute planning of what were then dormitory rooms. In early times the students slept in common and studied apart. Wykeham provided big rooms for four beds facing upon the quad, and small, separate studies at the back. This scheme also was followed in other plans. But the increasing luxury of college life led to a reversal of the use. The undergraduates claimed their own bedrooms, for which they used the small back rooms; and by the eighteenth century they expected each to have a large room as a living-room. This naturally involved a considerable expansion of the accommodation of the colleges; and hence it is that so many colleges have at some time added an extra storey to their buildings. It is a pity, for this addition always dwarfs the importance of the entrance-tower and increases the feeling of confinement. Without its third floor, the New College quadrangle would be marvellously spacious and the height of chapel and hall would be enhanced.

Wykeham set his lofty chapel and hall on the north side so as not to keep the sun from his quadrangle. He also put the two under one continuous roof to secure the harmonious unity which it was left for Sir George Gilbert Scott to interrupt. In his chapel Wykeham introduced the Perpendicular style, which was only conceived at Gloucester some fifty years before. He also devised the famous T-shaped plan adopted by so many colleges. By setting at right angles to the choirs a wide ante-chapel of almost equal size, he secured two advantages: first, he had an east wall long enough for a group of altars for private worship, and secondly he had a large room where the college could meet for theological debate or instruction without slighting the high altar, and where ceremonial processions could have space to form. Both parts of this chapel are noble pieces of Gothic. There is no east window, owing to the position of the hall adjoining. Its place is taken by a wall of sculptures. These were destroyed at the Reformation, and the present work was restored in accordance with Wykeham's design under the supervision of Gilbert Scott. The chapel roof has also undergone much change. Wyatt destroyed the original hammerbeam roof and made one of plaster; Scott in his turn destroyed this and most regrettably decided to substitute one of steeper pitch. The great west window of the ante-chapel embodies a remarkable design, painted on the glass after a cartoon by Sir Joshua Reynolds. The upper lights represent the Nativity and the Adoration, the lower lights represent the Virtues, a row of figures of somewhat buxom charm. The other windows of the ante-chapel contain extremely fine original glass, which only survived the ravages of the Reformation because the college pleaded that it had no money at the time to substitute plain glass.

Beyond the chapel to the west lie the incomparable cloisters, standing apart. Two years after the opening of New College William of Wykeham bought this extra plot of land to serve as a burial ground to the members of his foundation ; and in 1400 the cloister was consecrated. Nowhere in England do the years stand still as they do in this silent and holy spot. A single entrance, the shade of a single ilex, a single tower standing guard, a single window overlooking the solitude. In a corner stands a curious fire-engine, and round the walls are monuments—curious inscriptions to the memory of " Scroggs Goad " and many others. The tower was built by Wykeham as a belfry, to stand clear of the chapel ; but as it filled the place of one of the bastions in the city wall, he agreed to fortify it as well. During the Civil Wars it did service as a gunpowder-mill, while munitions were stored within the cloister.

From the great quad you reach the hall by a flight of stairs beneath another tower which balances the ante-chapel. This is the Muniment Tower, designed like that at Merton to keep marauders and incendiaries at bay. Its strongly barred windows still protect a collection of treasures which is well worth viewing. The hall, forming as it does a single range with the chapel, is of similar size but smaller height ; this also was considerably altered by Scott.

Leaving the quad by an archway on the east side, beneath the library, you come into an eighteenth-century court known as the Garden Quad, although it lacks a fourth side. This was added by William Bird about 1684, at which time there was a reaction against closed quadrangles, partly on hygienic grounds and partly as a matter of architectural fashion. Between this quad and the garden itself is a superb iron screen of the same date.

New College garden is something of a show place, on account of the fine stretch of the old wall which shelters it. When Wykeham bought his land in the north-east corner of the city wall, he was allowed to build upon it on the condition that he kept the wall in good repair. This stipulation is honoured to this day, with the result that the old defences are here seen in their perfection. At the permitted hours it is very agreeable to make the circuit of New College garden. The clump of trees in the centre of the lawn conceals the remains of a great mound erected here in Tudor times, when a mound was regarded as an amusing feature in an enclosed garden.

In summer you will find the garden well tenanted with studious and sedate young men. An air of decorum and regularity broods over lawn and trees and walls, and is exemplified in the familiar inscription over the iron gates : " Manners Makyth Man." The personality of the founder has made itself felt from generation to generation. A man who has been to Winchester is almost always recognisable by his modest and serious deportment; a man who has been to Winchester and New College in succession is frequently so modest and so serious that he may be overlooked entirely. Wykeham's foundations produce many distinguished civil servants, many bishops, many judges, many successful men in any safe and reputable walk in life. It cannot be said that they are nurseries of great political gifts, of demagogy, of military or naval glory. No Waterloos have been won on this trim and sheltered sward.

Until less than a century ago every scholarship or fellowship at New College was reserved to Winchester alone. The relaxation of this rule has brought a great expansion to the college. It has spread to the north of its wall, where if you care to look you will find a great block of buildings by Gilbert Scott, which are also a prominent disfigurement to Holywell Street beyond. New College is distinguished in every branch of university life, though it still adheres closely to the Winchester connection. A characteristic son of Wykeham's two foundations is the present Warden, Mr. H. A. L. Fisher, who is due to retire in the present year. His predecessor, Dr. Spooner, owned another sort of fame, having given birth to the " kinkering kongs " type of joke. Nor let us fail to do honour to an earlier warden, well named Dr. Shuttleworth. This witty and ingenious man contrived a famous apparatus by which decanters of port could be transported across the open end of a horseshoe table in the senior common room without human aid. An " inclined mahogany railroad " does the business, enabling a ceaseless clockwise circulation to be maintained. This labour-saving contrivance remains in daily use. If a Warden of Merton discovered the circulation of the blood, a Warden of New College helped it on its way.

And now to All Souls, across a gap of fifty years. The entrance to All Souls is in the High Street, where now a lethal flood of buses and bicycles hurtles past. Formerly it was the duty of the porter at All Souls at the beginning of each Michaelmas term to sally into the High Street and pull up the weeds which had accumulated during the Long Vacation.

The front of All Souls has been refaced, but the small quadrangle within remains exactly as it was finished off in 1444. No extra storeys have been added here, and for the reason that All Souls is the only college which has never exceeded the scope of its founder's intentions. It was built for a warden and forty fellows; to-day it has a warden and fifty-four fellows. No such thing as an undergraduate disturbs its repose; whence its renown as a place of scholastic purity and refinement.

It is evident how closely the admirable plans of William of Wykeham were copied in this, the next college but one to be built

15 All Souls : the Hall Quad

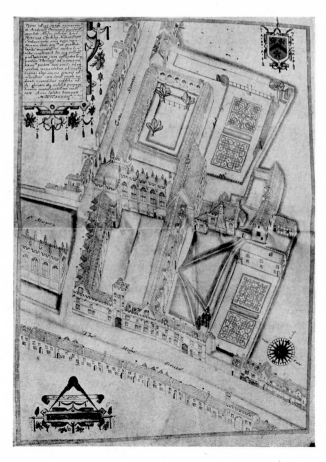

16 A Plan of All
Souls in 1598

17 St. Mary's from the North

after his.   Here is the enclosed quad ; here is the gateway tower ;
here is the T-shaped chapel ; here are the hall and chapel ranged
along the north side of the quad ; here are the separate staircases,
independent and apart.

This chapel is simply a small edition of the other, reredos and
all.   This reredos is also a substitute for one destroyed at the
Reformation on account of its profane profusion of statues.   When
the sculptures were gone, the wall was plastered up and a voluptu-
ous painting of the Resurrection, " full of nakeds," took their
place.   But in Victorian times a praiseworthy effort was made
(again by Sir George Gilbert Scott) to reconstruct the old masterpiece.   Alas, though the money was there, the talent was not ; and
the present work, for which the fellows of the college lent themselves as models, is merely grotesque.   There is a hammerbeam
roof, which gives an idea of what New College chapel lost by
Wyatt's reconstruction ; and the classical screen, falsely ascribed
to Wren, was certainly fortunate to escape the pure Gothic zeal
of Scott.

The hall of All Souls was originally a small affair set at right
angles to the east wall of the chapel ; but an ingenious warden,
Dr. George Clarke, rebuilt it on the true Wykehamist plan in 1729,
extending the lines and proportions of the chapel in an easterly
direction.   He also contrived a charming buttery for the fellows
to have lunch in.   Nor was this the limit of Clarke's admirable
innovations.   In 1710 there died one Christopher Codrington, a
fellow of All Souls who resided in Barbados.   He left a large
collection of books to the college, and Dr. Clarke set to work to
provide a room for them.   Having formed a single unit of the
chapel and hall, it was decided to balance this with an enormous
library as big as the two put together.   This scheme provided two
sides for a new and spacious quadrangle, which is reached by a
passage underneath the chapel.

It is not certain at what stage of the enterprise the assistance of
Nicholas Hawksmoor was called in.   Some of the fellows thought
that these ambitious schemes of their talented Warden afforded a
good occasion to demolish the whole college and start afresh on
more commodious lines.   Hawksmoor had lately done as much for
Queen's next door ; but to his credit he set his face against the
destruction of All Souls.   What he did was to complete Clarke's
excellent work by shaping it into a new quadrangle based upon the
Codrington library.   These were the days of open quadrangles, so
Hawksmoor stopped short at three sides and joined up the fourth
with a piazza.   The whole composition is much ridiculed, particularly the mock-Gothic towers ; but of course in Hawksmoor's
day the thread of the Gothic tradition had been wholly lost.   His
compromise is odd, but none of it is in the least offensive except
to strict rules.   Inside, the library is more like a cathedral ; it is

open to all graduates of the university, being particularly rich in legal books; among its treasures is a large collection of original drawings by Sir Christopher Wren, who was a fellow of the college. As a young man Wren designed a large sundial to go on the south wall of the chapel : this was moved on to the wall of the Codrington when it was built.

As you walk through All Souls you may observe some very familiar or illustrious names on the little boards at the bottom of each staircase. For the fellows of All Souls are a very remarkable collection of men. Every year one or two of the most brilliant undergraduates are chosen by examination, and are given £300 a year for five years without any obligation to reside at all. To most of them this bounty is merely a means to success in the law or elsewhere, and their rooms in college are occupied only at week-ends. Others remain in Oxford to pursue researches of unfathomable depth. At the end of the five years those who do not reside are reduced to £50, while those who remain in Oxford continue at the full rate until they marry. Other fellows are elected in later life in recognition of some special distinction or become members *ex officio* on appointment to one of a number of professorial chairs. Thus the senior common room at All Souls is distinguished above all others by the great brains which meet there and by the singular unfruitfulness of their collaboration. Among lawyers, Sir John Simon, the Master of the Rolls, and the Attorney-General are all members ; among churchmen, the Bishop of Gloucester. But it is not these who make the running. Rather is it the Editor of *The Times* and his circle of associates—men whom the public voice has called to no office and entrusted with no responsibility. These individuals elect to consider themselves as powers behind the scenes. The duty of purveying honest news is elevated in their eyes into the prerogative of dictating opinion. It is at All Souls that they meet to decide just how little they will let their readers know ; and their newspaper has been called the *All Souls Parish Magazine*.

All Souls was not always thus elevated above the intellectual level of mankind. Its founder, Chichele, had made it a provision that all who were related to him should have first claim to fellowships. Till the statute was abolished these " founder's kin " made full use of the privilege ; and they were a mixed lot. Here is a bit of scandal of 1675. The university press, writes one Humphrey Prideaux, " hath been imployed about printeing Aretin's *Postures*. The gentlemen of All Souls had got them engraved, and had imployed our presse to print them off. The time that was chosen for the worke was the eveneing after 4, Mr. Dean after that time never useing to come to the theator ; but last night, beeing imployed the other part of the day, he went not thither till the work was begun. How he tooke to find his presse workeing at such an imployment I leave you to immagin. The prints and the plates he hath seased, and threatens the owners of them with expulsion ; and I thinke they would deserve it were they of any other colledge than All Souls, but there I will allow them to be vertuous that are bawdy only in pictures. That colledge in my esteem is a scandalous place."

Again in 1707 we find " an abominable riot committed in All Souls College." It was an odd form of riot, however, consisting in two fellows of Whig views celebrating the anniversary of King Charles's execution with a dinner of woodcocks, " whose heads they cut off, in contempt of the memory of the blessed martyr." The cook, it seems, had refused to serve them with calves' heads, which would have been more insulting still. How far-fetched and remote it seems ; yet by Oxford's standards it was just the other day. As you leave All Souls, you will see that the High Street frontages terminate in a fine Queen Anne house, built by Dr. Clarke for the use of the Warden. This house was finished only the year before this abominable riot, and its still damp rooms must have reverberated with the scandal.

Renaissance Oxford
as it was

THE NEXT STAGE IN OXFORD'S DEVELOPMENT COVERS THE period when the Renaissance dawned in England, a hundred years after it had reached its zenith in Italy, and the period when England first broke away from Rome. It starts about the year 1450, when Merton Tower was raised, and ends with the death in 1558 of Bloody Mary. During this period five more colleges were founded, the last which saw the light beneath the auspices of the Church of Rome.

Another man of outstanding personality now takes the place of Wykeham. This is William Waynflete. Born in 1395, he was one of the earliest of all the thousands who have progressed from Winchester to New College. He became in turn head master of Winchester, fellow of Eton, Provost of Eton, Bishop of Winchester, and Lord Chancellor. Eton owes him much, but Oxford owes him more. For following in the footsteps of the benefactor to whom he owed his start in life, he founded the College of St. Mary Magdalen in 1458. Though there is no statutory connection between the two bodies, the lilies of Eton adorn the Magdalen coat of arms; and Magdalen, which has always maintained a foremost place among Oxford colleges, has claimed at every period a fair quota of Etonians.

There is about Magdalen a certain spaciousness and serenity which seems to breathe the very spirit of its age. The clash of arms was giving way to the conflict of philosophers, and all over Europe the bars and battlements were being taken down and the windows were being opened to the light and air of a new knowledge and understanding. The " wars for the crown of France " were over ; travel abroad was safer than it was in England ; men felt that a new and more generous age had begun. Waynflete was not afraid to set his college beyond the east gate and outside the shelter of the city walls. His gardens and his park ran down to the undefended river. He built no stronghold against a half-savage mob ; he fortified no belfry against a civil war. Instead, soon after his death his college raised the tower that greets you upon

18   The Approach to Oxford, 1814 (*Ackermann's " Oxford "*)

19   Magdalen Tower from Merton
Garden

Magdalen bridge, that exquisite miracle in stone which James I so truly called " the most absolute building in Oxford." In 1504 they opened this tower by giving a concert upon the leads ; and the voices of the choristers were raised to greet not only a new spring and a new peal of bells, but also the high hopes of a new century. Men like Erasmus, Grocyn, Colet, and Thomas More, returning from travel all full of the new Greek learning, met and disputed to the first music of the Magdalen bells.

Still we are concerned with benefactors who drew their wealth and their precepts from the Mother Church. But the renaissance of Oxford is deeply indebted to a royal lover of learning. Far more than the lore of the monks, the new classical learning was dependent upon the dissemination of books ; and at the present the books of the university were all contained in one room above the Congregation House. Its first great library was the gift of Duke Humphrey of Gloucester, the youngest son of Henry IV. " Good Duke Humphrey," as those who lived upon his bounty called him, was very fond of reading, and he left his books to Oxford. But he did far more than this ; for he gave money to the university to start a reconstruction of a drastic kind.

Nobody knows the number of the students at Oxford in the fifteenth century, but some estimates make them up to three thousand. Only a fraction of these resided in the nine colleges that existed before Magdalen. It is said that there were no fewer than eighty-four halls of various sizes. And innumerable students merely lodged in the town. This want of organisation in the residential system was matched in the educational sphere. A " school " could be set up by anybody, genius or charlatan, who cared to try it. There was a street of schools, in which more than thirty teachers competed to attract custom. It was clearly time to introduce some regularity into the system, and the benefactions of Duke Humphrey were employed for this purpose. As early as 1439 a central School of Arts had been built ; four years later the university approached the Duke for funds to build a School of Divinity. He did not live to see it ; and the work went slowly, because the King took off his builders to complete the great chapel at Eton. But in 1480 the work was done, and Duke Humphrey is commemorated by a building of a double utility. Lectures were to be given in the divinity school itself ; the room above it housed his famous library. Thus did the university acquire its first important building.

Within a stone's throw of the new divinity school there stood a famous hall whose history well illustrates the vicissitudes of the earlier times. The knocker of this hall was in the shape of a bronze lion's head, from which the name of Brazen Nose Hall had come to be applied. In the year 1334 the students of this hall, dissatisfied by some part of the university's teaching or discipline,

4

20 (*opposite*) : The Cathedral Nave, from a drawing by Thomas Malton (1804)

left Oxford in a body, taking their precious knocker with them. They made their way to Stamford, where apparently some sort of educational centre existed; and there they reconstituted their society. The Oxford authorities were so furious at this secession that they laid Stamford under an interdict; they insisted that every candidate for a Mastership of Arts should swear never to give or attend a lecture at Stamford. This oath was not eliminated until the year 1827, centuries after poor Stamford had lost all cultural pretensions; while in 1509 the parent hall had become Brasenose College, thus ranking eleventh among the foundations of Oxford. Sir Richard Sutton, its co-founder with the Bishop of Lincoln, was the first lay founder of a college.

Most men in the Oxford of this time were aware that they stood on the verge of a great change. All these printed books, all this Continental travel, all this reading of scripture in the Greek caused much misgiving as to the sufficiency of the monastic life. When the great world produced such a generous bounty of piety and learning, men looked with a more contemptuous eye upon the refugees of the cloister. The feeling of the times is well expressed in a short fragment of recorded talk. Richard Foxe, yet another Bishop of Winchester, wished to apply some of the excessive emoluments of that see to some new work in Oxford, and he discussed his plans with his friend Hugh Oldham, Bishop of Exeter, who thus expressed himself: " What, my Lord, shall we build houses and provide livelihoods for a company of bussing monks whose end and fall we ourselves may live to see; no, no, it is more meet that we should have care to provide for the increase of learning, and for such as by their learning shall do good in the Church and the Commonwealth." Foxe fell in with this vigorous advice; and he and Oldham between them became the founders of the college of Corpus Christi in the year 1516. It was expressly provided in the statutes of this college that no member could assume monastic vows and remain on the foundation. Professors of Greek and Latin were attached to the foundation and the fellows and scholars were encouraged to travel abroad. Thus Corpus became at the very start what it has remained to this day, a shrine of classical learning at its highest.

Foxe did not quite live to see the end and fall of the bussing monks, but he came within a few years of it. In truth the monks were falling fast when Henry VIII administered the last blows to them. Long before he thought of looting the monastic houses upon principle, many of them were empty and others existed for the benefit of a dozen or half a dozen occupants. It was no impiety in Cardinal Wolsey to attack these useless bodies in the interest of Oxford's next and greatest foundation.[1]

[1] For example, All Souls, a century earlier, was largely endowed by Archbishop Chichele from the revenues of suppressed priories.

Wolsey was an Oxford man who had put his learning to good use in the Church and in the Commonwealth. He was in turn a scholar, fellow, and bursar of Magdalen, and secretary to Bishop Foxe. At the age of forty he became Lord Chancellor and a Cardinal. Some ten years later he obtained a papal bull entitling him to suppress and take over St. Frideswide's Priory and any other religious houses which had less than seven remaining members. In exercise of this power he mopped up some forty institutions, sent their monks elsewhere, and set about the grandiose scheme of "Cardinal College" in the year 1525, on the site where the sainted virgin's soul had received the benefit of eight centuries of prayer.

Rather to the annoyance of historians, Wolsey never fails to seize the imagination. His stupendous fortune, palaces, and banquets remain in the memory while more important aspects of foreign, religious, or domestic policy escape. So it is with Wolsey's work at Oxford. All that has been written about the new learning may be very dull, but "Cardinal College" is an unfailing thrill. Down comes the great man, with his red hat, his papal bull, and his forty-two effete houses. Away goes St. Frideswide's, its refectories, its dormitories, even a part of its Norman church. And up there springs in its place—a kitchen, a gigantic, a truly Wolseyan kitchen. Oxford had its first great laugh over Wolsey's kitchen, whose immense proportions foreshadowed not only the scale but also the wealth and luxury of the new college. Next they marked out an enormous quad, and the city wall was knocked down to make way for a hall far larger than any Oxford had yet seen, and men talked about a chapel on the other side which was to be the rival of King's College Chapel at Cambridge. Avenues were being planted in the meadows, and money was being poured out like water, when suddenly the great man fell and everything was taken from him. This was in 1529, so that "Cardinal College" had four years of life before King Henry confiscated it. But the fallen Wolsey wrote to the King and begged him to spare "the poor College"; and three years later, it saw the light again as "King Henry VIII's College." Under this name it staggered on for several years, till in a general loot of likely foundations the King suppressed his own. Finally, not long before his death, Henry VIII decided upon a new arrangement which has lasted ever since. Having set up the new reformed diocese of Oxford, he turned the last Abbot of Osney into the first Bishop of Oxford, and gave him St. Frideswide's as his cathedral, by the name of the Cathedral Church of Christ. But since St. Frideswide's was surrounded by Wolsey's unfinished buildings, he also reconstituted the former college under the name of the "House of Christ" or Christ Church, and put it in charge of the Dean of the cathedral. And finally by way of benefaction he added to it the neighbouring properties of Peckwater and Canterbury.

This last reconstitution took place in 1546, and a few months later Henry VIII was dead. Though he ranks legally as the parent of Oxford's greatest foundation, he despoiled the university in other ways. Commissioners sent down by Thomas Cromwell to Oxford were expressly warned by the King to keep their rapacious hands off his own college; but they did suppress three of the old monastic colleges—St. Bernard's, Durham, and Gloucester. Under Henry's successor Oxford fared even worse. A fresh lot of commissioners arrived in 1549 and 1550, and in the name of the infant Edward VI they indulged a Protestant orgy, pillaging the chapels, and, above all, destroying the libraries. Duke Humphrey's library, so proudly housed not a century before, was wholly destroyed. Most of the valuable manuscripts were burnt, and even the very shelves were taken down and sold by these good Calvinists.

Needless to say, there was no new building done in Oxford while such lovers of learning as these held power. But another three years brought back the old religion under the doughty auspices of Bloody Mary. She and Cardinal Pole lost no time in getting even with the time-servers of the last two reigns; and Oxford came into the limelight once more when in 1554 there arrived from the Tower of London three distinguished prisoners in the persons of Archbishop Cranmer and Bishops Latimer and Ridley. They had been sent to Oxford to defend their views before an assembly of divines, and this they attempted to do in April 1554; but in the circumstances it is not strange that they came off second best. They were sent back to wait another eighteen months, pending the decision of their fate, in a prison called Bocardo which spanned the Cornmarket at the North Gate beside St. Michael's Tower. In the next year both Latimer and Ridley were tried in St. Mary's Church and condemned to be burnt at the stake; and a few days later burnt they were, outside the north wall and opposite to Balliol. A small cross let into the roadway and a taxi-rank now mark the place of their martyrdom. It is said that Cranmer watched their sufferings from the window of Bocardo; for with him, who had originally received his archbishopric from Rome, a more formal procedure had to be adopted. He too was tried in St. Mary's, but by a representative of the Pope, who then excommunicated him. Months later he was taken to the new Cathedral to be degraded; and finally he was taken to St. Mary's once more to recant his heresies. Six written recantations had failed to avert the death sentence, and Cranmer knew he was to be burnt immediately after his appearance in the church. He would not be further humiliated, and he mounted the platform and withdrew his writings with the famous prayer that his right hand might be the first burnt. So he died on the same spot as the two others, an honourable end to a not very edifying life.

Later generations of Puritans have seen to it that the burning

24

of the bishops should not be forgotten; but Oxford owes more to the reign of Bloody Mary than a solitary *auto-da-fé*. The year 1555 saw the rebirth of two of the suppressed monastic colleges in unmonastic guise. Two wealthy Catholic laymen, Sir Thomas Pope and Sir Thomas White, purchased respectively the properties of Durham College and St. Bernard's, and founded the new colleges of Trinity and St. John's. These were the last colleges to originate under the old religion. In 1558 Queen Mary died, and thenceforward Oxford has slept securely beneath the peaceful shelter of the established Church of England.

22 (*opposite*) : The fan-vaulted Staircase
to Christ Church Hall

Renaissance Oxford
as it is

O N THIS SECOND ITINERARY IT WILL BE MOST APPROPRIATE TO start at Magdalen, as the birthplace in Oxford of the new age. It is certainly the most beautiful of all the colleges, and preserves in every feature and in its stately atmosphere a feeling very akin to Eton among schools. Its name, incidentally, is pronounced Maudlin.

It is an untidy college. Fronting the road is a row of buildings which incorporate some bits of an old Hospital of St. John which stood there when Waynflete bought the site. Within the low entrance you will find a straggling courtyard, known as St. John's Quad after the old hospital. In the corner to your right is an open-air pulpit from which a sermon is preached on St. John the Baptist's day ; the congregation used to seat themselves on a floor of rushes below. Adjoining is the west window of the chapel, which seems to have been so set as a termination to the view down the High Street. The west door of the chapel is rarely used ; you must gain access by a side door beneath the adjoining muniment tower. This chapel was finished some twenty years after the college had been founded, that is to say, a hundred years after New College chapel ; but you will once again observe how closely the Wykeham plan is followed. Here again is the spacious ante-chapel set at right angles to the choir and the great east wall without a window. But beyond the bare plan, there is little inside it that is old. Wyatt destroyed the ancient roof, just as he did at New College ; and in the 1830's the rest of the interior was gutted. The old embellishments were put up to auction in the college stables ; and what you see now is the work of an architect named Cottingham. Even the remarkable glass in the ante-chapel is only Jacobean. But one treasure Magdalen chapel has always preserved, and that is its music. The choral services are famous even in this musical city. So keen is the pride of Magdalen in this tradition that one choirmaster in Elizabethan times got into

26

23   Magdalen : St. John's Quad

24   Magdalen : the Cloister

25   Bishop King's Palace

trouble when he " captured a poor boy at Malmesbury and brought him in chains to Oxford " to serve as a chorister.

The hall, as at New College, stands in line with the chapel and to the east ; it is reached along one side of the cloisters and up a flight of stairs. It contains some good linen-fold panelling dated 1541 and a Jacobean screen ; the roof was here also destroyed by Wyatt.

Magdalen cloisters cannot compare with those at New College ; their layout is far more reminiscent of those at Eton. Just as at Eton, they are dominated by a single entrance tower ; here it is called the Founder's Tower, and a lovely Perpendicular block it is. The arch below has not for centuries been used as an entrance ; and the great room above it, intended for the head of the college, now constitutes part of a suite reserved for visiting royalty. Magdalen numbers among its members the Duke of Windsor, who was in residence as an undergraduate from 1912 to 1914 ; but though he visited the college when he was King, the occasion could hardly be described as royal. Another feature of the cloisters is the array of carved animals which surmount the buttresses. The story goes that when one of these figures was being repaired, the under-graduates bribed the sculptor to make it a likeness of the senior fellow, Dr. Ellerton, a remarkable character. So soon as the resemblance was noticed, the doctor commanded the sculptor to remove it by hollowing the cheeks and deepening the lines. Many years later he looked once more and found that he had grown to be the very image of the gargoyle.

To this same Dr. Ellerton we probably owe the present existence of this quadrangle. In the year 1822 he returned from a vacation to find that the north range was being busily demolished. Those were great days for rebuilding ; and some busybody, alleging that the old work was dangerous, had planned to open out the whole quadrangle. As it was, Dr. Ellerton's insistence saved the east wing ; the north side was rebuilt also, but in a less picturesque shape than formerly.

This was not the only narrow shave that Magdalen's old buildings have survived. As early as 1724 we find the excellent Hawksmoor writing to announce that he has plans for a whole new college at Magdalen, as the old buildings are " so decrepit." Apparently the fellows thought so, too, for they allowed a certain Edward Holdsworth, who was one of their number, to prepare a grandiose scheme of vast classical quadrangles on the lines of what Hawksmoor actually carried out at Queen's. They actually built one wing of Holdsworth's design in 1733, and you will find it facing you if you leave the cloisters by a narrow passage or tunnel on the north side, that is to say, opposite the chapel and hall. Here is an extremely eighteenth-century corner of Oxford. To your left an immense plane tree ; to your right a very fine herbaceous border fringing a branch-stream of the Cherwell ; in front a wide expanse of grass and the solid plain front of the New Buildings, as they have ever since been called. They are not one of Oxford's masterpieces ; but the rooms inside them are ample and comfortable, and on the other side they command a quite enchanting view of Magdalen Grove, which is a really very extensive deer-park, cool, lush, and dark with elms. The Grove, which visitors may not enter, is one of the features which give Magdalen its feeling of grandeur. Christ Church has its meadows, Worcester its lake, and Merton its fields ; but only Magdalen has a park.

Any visitor is at liberty, on the other hand, to cross the little bridge beside New Buildings and explore the Walks. These constitute a complete circuit of an island meadow, just about a mile round and extremely pretty. The northern section of the pathway goes by the name of Addison's Walk, having been frequented by the sanctimonious Joseph when he was a fellow of Magdalen in Queen Anne's reign. But if you want historic associations, Magdalen can go better than Addison. Gibbon had rooms in the New Buildings just twenty years after they were built : what he thought about Magdalen and about Oxford in general will be told elsewhere. In Magdalen Hall one day in 1649 Cromwell and Fairfax were entertained at dinner, and afterwards they played a game of bowls ; Cromwell, a lover of music, took a fancy to the fine organ in the chapel, and, like the true Nazi that he was, carried it away for his own pleasure at Hampton Court. A few years earlier and Charles I had been paying many visits to Magdalen to mount the Tower and scan the slopes of Shotover for signs of his enemies ; while Prince Rupert's artillery had been set up in the Grove beneath. It was over Magdalen Bridge that Charles made his last dash for London, leaving Oxford in the disguise of a servant. And farther back yet there is a curious notice in the Annals of the University for 1586 : " Certain Scholars of Magdalen College stealing deer in the Forest of Shotover belonging to the King, one of them . . . was carried before the Lord Norreys and by him imprisoned." Lord Norreys duly visited Oxford for the quarter sessions, and lodged at the Bear Inn by All Saint's Church, where some of the scholars assaulted his retinue, but were beaten back by Norreys' son Maximilian " as far as St. Mary's Church." However, " Binks the Lord's Keeper was sorely wounded." When the time came for Norreys to leave Oxford by the eastern road, the scholars were ordered to stay in their colleges. " But the Scholars of Magdalen College being not able to pocket these affronts went up privately to the top of their Tower and waiting till he should pass towards Ricot sent down a shower of stones that they had picked up, upon him and his retinue, wounding some and endangering others of their lives." His Lordship, who barely escaped with his life, was " with much ado pacified by the sages of the University."

This tower of theirs is certainly one of the jewels of Oxford. Its subtly tapered form and placid detail characterise late Gothic at its best. It is worth while to climb it to the top, though you will see a view of miles of unspeakable suburb out to the east where Charles saw the slopes of Headington and his forest of Shotover. This tower was started after Waynflete's death, and completed in 1504. From that day to this it has been customary each year on May Day to greet the sunrise with a concert on the roof of the tower. Formerly this concert was a two hours' performance of " catches and instrumental music " ; but since the eighteenth century it has been nothing but a Latin anthem chanted into the wind by a phalanx of blue-nosed choristers, while the girls of St. Hilda's, dreamy but tense, hug their thick mufflers and listen from the bridge below.

Before leaving Magdalen, you may notice in the first quadrangle, by which you came in, a sort of doll's house, standing by itself and fairly reeking of antiquity. This is the Grammar Hall, relic of a preparatory school attached to Magdalen, which has now so much bettered itself that it has moved to the other side of Magdalen Bridge. The small scale and advanced decay of this particular block make it appear older than its surroundings. On either side of it are modern Gothic buildings—to the right the President's lodging, to the left St. Swithin's quad, both built by the scholarly and tasteful partnership of Messrs. Bodley and Garner some fifty years ago. Beyond St. Swithin's quad is a still newer block built in strict conformity by the present Sir Giles Gilbert Scott some ten years ago. There is also an archway, designed but not used as a gate, which Bodley and Garner substituted for an earlier work by Pugin, who in his turn replaced a massive portal built by Inigo Jones.

As you walk up the High Street from Magdalen, you will be able to enjoy some of the most celebrated views in Europe, as the wide curve exposes its stone panorama. On your left the East Gate Hotel marks the point where the city confines ended. Before you on the right-hand side is the great classical pile of Queen's. But just before you reach it, I would have you turn up Queen's Lane for a few yards and look in at St. Edmund Hall.

" Teddy Hall " has little history, but it fits in with the period of the renaissance very well. Being a Hall, it has no date for its foundation, since nobody ever founded it. At some time, long before the Reformation, it merely started itself. Its name is taken from Oxford's first saint, Edmund Rich of Abingdon, later Archbishop of Canterbury, who is supposed to have held his school on this site. The Hall was famous at a very early date as a Wyclifite centre. The actual house belonged to Osney Abbey ; so that when Henry VIII took away the property of Osney, the Hall found itself just a part of the plunder. From this predicament it was rescued by its wealthy neighbour Queen's. Queen's had for some time past appointed each successive Principal of St. Edmund Hall, though by custom rather than by right: now in 1557 they bought the freehold, and assumed the legal right to appoint a Principal. Their title recited the undertaking of Queen's that "henceforth and for ever they will preserve the aforesaid Hall and preserve it to literary uses." Beneath this kindly protectorate, St. Edmund Hall has flourished. The north range of buildings, which presents a charming front to the church-yard beyond, was built in 1596 : after the Restoration were built a chapel and library and hall. With all the characteristics of a college, "Teddy Hall" retained the status of a mere lodging-house. Finally, in the nineteenth century, there were only four Halls left in Oxford, and a Royal Commission of radical busy-bodies decided in 1877 that they should all be swallowed up by one or other of the colleges. So St. Alban Hall became part of Merton, St. Mary Hall part of Oriel, and New Inn Hall was abolished by Balliol. But St. Edmund Hall survived through the longevity of its Principal. It was thought that it would not be " done " to extinguish his Hall in his lifetime ; and by the time he died, people were less keen about the removal of anomalies. Lord Curzon, a great Chancellor of the University, championed the cause of this last Hall ; and in 1913 an Order in Council recognised its unique status. Since then it has trebled its membership ; now it has nearly 150 undergraduates, and they put up a good show in athletic competition with far larger bodies. In 1937, they cele-brated the seventh centenary of Edmund Rich's archiepiscopal appointment. The present Archbishop came down and opened a new block called Canterbury Buildings. At the same time Queen's College handed over their freehold and relinquished their legal rights over the Hall. Now it stands entirely on its own feet, lack-ing nothing but a founder. The reason why all the other Halls have gone under is that the colleges were endowed and they were not. St. Edmund Hall is still unendowed ; and lately it has issued a statement that it requires the fairly modest sum of £5000 a year. Here is a grand opportunity for some Wykeham or Waynflete of the present day to display his piety or celebrate his celibacy. I do not vouch that they will substitute his name for that of Edmund Rich, but they will make better use of the money than all the museum-curators and archæologists in the world.

Passing Queen's College and All Souls once more, you come to St. Mary's Church, whose spire is of the Middle Ages and the rest of it nearly two centuries younger. The church itself was built between 1460 and 1500, that is to say, at the same time as Mag-dalen. It is a very handsome Perpendicular church, and gains in effect from the fact that so many of the windows have been spared the insertion of stained glass.

26   St. Mary's : the Baroque South Porch

27, 28   Two Views of Christ Church Hall

It has been described how the two bishops were tried in this church after their unsuccessful dispute in the Divinity School, and how Cranmer here recanted his recantations. There is a legend that on one of the pillars you can see the marks where his platform was erected : but this is all nonsense. The truth is that St. Mary's has been put to all sorts of odd uses. It was always the university church ; and until the Sheldonian Theatre was built, St. Mary's was used as a theatre as well as a church. Here the Mayor came for five centuries to atone for St. Scholastica's day. Here came Queen Elizabeth to listen to three solid days of academic discourse, and to wind them up with a Latin harangue. Here were held the degree-giving ceremonies, accompanied by a great deal of gross buffoonery. One way and another, dozens of platforms must have been erected in St. Mary's besides Cranmer's.

Now the church is used entirely as a church, except that in 1936, when the Sheldonian was under repair, it was used once more for the degree-giving ceremony. On Sundays in term the university sermons are preached here. They were a great draw in the days of the Tractarians, when the eloquence of Newman and Keble shook the university to its foundations : but nowadays they attract less attentive audiences.

The entrance porch of St. Mary's, as you will observe, is not of the Perpendicular period ; far from it. This fulsome specimen of the baroque was added, somewhat astonishingly, a full hundred years before the real era of baroque : but the story of that porch belongs so inevitably to the next chapter that it should be left for then.

Down Oriel Street, which is opposite St. Mary's, you come to Corpus Christi, a miniature college squeezed between Merton and Christ Church, though it has now some modern extensions by Sir Thomas Jackson on the other side of the road. Corpus, as has been said, was founded in 1516, and the whole of the front quad was built within the next twelve years. It is small and bare, with a curious mathematical sundial in the centre. The small chapel is reached by the far left corner ; its altarpiece is said to be a Rubens, and at the west end is a delightful gallery-pew which opens out of the library on the first floor. Beyond the chapel are a cloister and some eighteenth-century rooms whose handsome elevations are marred by the extreme decay of the stonework. Though Corpus is a very distinguished college in its scholastic tradition, it is not really a very interesting college to visit. It has one outstanding historical association in that a Dr. Reynolds, who was President of Corpus, was one of the translators of the Authorised Version, and entertained his collaborators here.

Next door to tiny Corpus lies immense Christ Church, of which the Canterbury Gate adjoins. This gate, however, is not always open, and will lead you into the least historical portion of the college. A more satisfactory approach is by Christ Church Meadows, which you can reach by the pathway which divides Corpus from Merton. Across the Meadows runs the Broad Walk, an immemorial avenue of elms. Another avenue runs southwards to the Thames bank. Where these two avenues meet there stands a vast and prickly pile of brick, well clothed in merciful creepers, which is the Meadow Building of Christ Church, the work of one Thomas Deane in 1863. These buildings present a second subsidiary entrance to Christ Church : but I would ask you to carry on to the end of the Broad Walk, which has quite lately been extended right along to St. Aldate's by one of those ingenious schemes which widen our streets at the same time as they commemorate our wars. As you come out on to the street, there is opposite you a remarkable Tudor domestic building, whose gables, woodwork, and plasterwork are all very perfect of their kind. This is called Bishop King's Palace, and is reputed to have been used for a short period by Robert King, when Henry VIII transmuted him from last Abbot of Osney into first Bishop of Oxford. It is now the residence of Monsignor Ronald Knox, the Catholic Chaplain to the university.

The southern end of the frontage of Christ Church on to St. Aldate's roughly marks the position of the old south gate of the city. Brewer Street opposite actually ran beneath the city wall. Facing little Pembroke stands one of Oxford's incomparable architectural treasures, Tom Tower, the joint work of Wolsey and Sir Christopher Wren. What sort of gateway Wolsey planned, nobody knows. He built the curious and elaborate turrets at either side, as high as the level of the adjoining balustrades : between them he foreshadowed a great oriel window. In all probability he meant to carry out some soaring conception such as Lupton's Tower at Eton : but the work was stopped at the time of his fall. The turrets were covered with makeshift lead roofs, and the great porch itself was left open to the sky for over a century. It was not until 1681 that Sir Christopher Wren was commissioned to complete the work. In the confidence of his great genius, he set aside the formal Tudor tower, and made play with the " ogee " form in capping the twin turrets as they stood, abandoning the oriel for a great recessed window, and carrying the central mass up to an octagonal bell-chamber. He also built an uncommonly fine fan-vault over the actual entrance-space.

Attempts were made to induce Wren to house an observatory in his tower, but he wisely refused. Instead it contains the great bell from which it takes its name, Great Tom, once the giant bell of Osney Abbey. At the time when this bell was recast and hung here, Christ Church had 101 scholars ; and every evening at five past nine the bell strikes out 101 strokes. At that sound every college in Oxford closes its gates, and thereafter admits only those

29, 30   Christ Church : the mediæval kitchen (*above*) in 1814 (*Ackermann's "Oxford"*) and (*below*) to-day

31   Christ Church Hall (*Ackermann's " Oxford "*)

32   Staircase, Christ Church : from a drawing by Thomas Rowlandson

who have lawful business. The tolling of Great Tom is like a symbol of the predominance of Christ Church over the university. It is easily the most important, the most delightful of all Oxford's foundations. It has the largest revenues, it provides the best food and the most spacious rooms, it sends forth the most successful alumni of any college. Yet it is not strictly a college at all. It is a solecism to speak of " Christ Church College " ; for by its foundation it was named simply "Aedes Christi," the Church or House of Christ ; and colloquially it is always spoken of as just " the House." Its head is a Dean ; its disciplinary authorities are not Deans, but " Censors " ; and its Fellows are " Students."

Tom Quad magnificently represents the grandeur and arrogance of the House and its splendid founder. Nearly a hundred yards square, it wholly dwarfs the ancient spire of the Cathedral tucked away in the far corner. Wolsey intended Tom Quad to be even grander than it is now. It was to be circled by a cloister, as the springers in the walls are meant to indicate, though they were in fact touched up by Sir George Gilbert Scott. Its north side was to be the site of a lofty chapel, intended to rival the superb chapel of King's at Cambridge ; and this in spite of the presence of a full-blown Cathedral already at hand. Wolsey did not live to build the north side of the Quad, which was completed a little before Tom Tower. Nor did he build the low square tower in the south-east corner ; this was raised about thirty feet not sixty years ago, in order to house the bells of the Cathedral. The work was well done by those skilful practitioners of the Gothic revival, Messrs. Bodley and Garner ; but it is a pity that they thought fit to put pinnacles on the hall, which had till then been crowned by a classical balustrade which continued to the very corner of the block.

Another feature of Tom Quad which Wolsey never knew is the pool in the centre, known as " Mercury " from the statue which adorns it. This little fountain has served a valuable purpose for many generations. In other colleges, those who refuse to conform with the prevailing standards of decency are solemnly " debagged," or relieved of their trousers. At the House the cry is to " Put him in Mercury ! " and the waters of Mercury have wrought many miraculous spiritual cures.[1]

Christ Church Hall is reached by the arch beneath Bodley's bell-tower. Here will be found a great stone stairway, folded round a single column ; and resting on the column is one of the most remarkable specimens of fan-vaulting in the whole world. Remarkable not only for its effect but in its origin ; for it was built in the 1630's, some two centuries after the era of fan-vaulting, by a London stonemason of whom about all we know is that his

---

[1] Robert Harley, Earl of Oxford, gave the statue of Queen Anne which faces Mercury from the inner side of Tom Tower.

name was Smith. How Wolsey would have delighted in this splendid piece of work.

At the head of these stairs is the Hall, undoubtedly the finest in Oxford, with its wide hammerbeam roof and the tall vaulted bay which lights its dais. Some of the woodwork and glass is of more recent dates ; but the space and dignity of the room are just what they were when Henry VIII banqueted here, after his refoundation of the House, or when Charles I used to dine here during the Civil Wars, and to assemble his loyal followers about him. This hall is also particularly rich in portraits. Every college has its treasures of this kind, which for some reason are always displayed in the appropriate eating-place. In the dingiest halls you will find Reynolds and Lely hidden away. But Christ Church has an incomparable collection, including a triple portrait by Lely, a Kneller of John Locke, a profusion of Gainsborough and Reynolds, and a Romney of John Wesley.

Beyond the hall is the well-known kitchen which caused so many jokes at Wolsey's expense. It is a favourite sight—a vast workshop full of massive implements and enormous fireplaces in which electric cookers now sizzle. The other passage leading from Mr. Smith's stairway conducts you to the ancient cloister, some of which belongs to the old St. Frideswide's, and so beyond to the horrific Meadow Buildings.

All the remainder of the Christ Church buildings belongs to later periods and later benefactors, of whom the most famous were the two Doctors Fell. Everybody knows the tag about " I do not like thee, Dr. Fell " ; but this epigram was apparently composed by an undergraduate in fulfilment of an imposition. There is no reason to suppose that anyone disliked either of the Doctors at all. Samuel Fell the elder was Dean of Christ Church in the reign of Charles I, and died of a broken heart upon the execution of that king, whom he must have come to know well during the Civil Wars. It was he who commissioned Smith to glorify his staircase. John Fell his son was Dean and later Bishop as well throughout the reign of Charles II.[1] These two good Anglicans completed Tom Quad between them. Wren's tower was built ; the north side was added in harmony with the others ; the whole quad was crowned by a graceful balustrade, which survives on the street front, though on the interior it has been scrapped in favour of fake battlements. The north range was dignified by a small tower of its own, once known as " Kill-Canon Tower." This is because Tom Quad accommodates no undergraduates, but only the Canons of the Cathedral ; ʌnd the north-easterly draughts

---

[1] John Locke, the philosopher, was student (i.e. a fellow) of Christ Church from start to finish of the same reign. He made himself objectionable to the Crown by his association with the unscrupulous Shaftesbury ; and in spite of the good offices of his friend Fell, he had in the end to be dismissed.

admitted by this entrance were held to be fatal to their sheltered constitutions.

Leaving Tom Quad by this same tower, beneath a statue of the younger Fell, you come to a highly formal and regular eighteenth-century quadrangle, which has lately been refaced with new stone. This is Peckwater Quadrangle, named after the inn which Henry VIII gave to the foundation. It was begun in 1705, the money being given by a Canon Radcliffe and the design that of Dean Aldrich, an excellent amateur architect who did great things for Oxford. The rooms in " Peck " are as spacious and ample as the design suggests, and their arrangement shows how very far ideas had changed about the comfort of the undergraduates. Now there is a tendency to revert to mediæval simplicity ; an attempt is being made to introduce the hateful " bed-sitter." But " Peck," with its wide staircases and tall rooms, remains the model of what an Oxford quad should be.

The Library which fills the open side of Peckwater is also the work of an unprofessional architect, that same Dr. Clarke whose work we have seen at All Souls. Begun only ten years later than the quadrangle itself, it is a far more massive and showy design, though its present rather oppressive effect might be mitigated if it also received the refacing which it so badly needs. To judge the building properly, one must remember that the ground floor was first intended to constitute an open piazza as at Trinity College, Cambridge. This was the classical formula for libraries. From Merton onwards, every library earlier than the Codrington was housed on an upper floor for fear of damp ; and the eighteenth century improved this notion by planning open cloisters and porticos to occupy the vacant ground floor. This was the intention not only here, but at Queen's and at the Radcliffe Camera itself. But the books always overflowed their shelves, and damp or no damp, the space below was always filled in the end.

It is very well worth while to enter this great library. On the ground floor are some interesting marbles, a varied collection of paintings, mostly Florentine, and Wolsey's red hat. The stair-case is a graceful elliptical design. The upper room, the library itself, is a splendid room in every respect—in its proportions, in its furnishing, and particularly in its sumptuous ceiling.

There remains but one corner of Christ Church to explore. Canterbury Quad, alongside of Peckwater, is a group designed by Wyatt about 1780 to frame the east end of the library. It also provides a worthy side entrance from Merton Street and Oriel Street.

Such is " the House," which is bigger, better, richer, and cheaper than any college in Oxford. The tremendous personality which appears in its buildings appears also in its personnel. Its deans have been illustrious and well paid,[1] its undergraduates illustrious and well born. In a single century it educated Canning, Peel, Gladstone, Salisbury, and Rosebery. It has a strong connection with Westminster School, dating from the foundation by Queen Elizabeth of a number of close scholarships. A large number of Etonians also go up to the House. The life is easygoing and tolerant ; the company is intelligent and gay. To crown all, the college revenues are well over £100,000 a year.

[1] Dr. Gaisford was a great Greek scholar as well as Dean of Christ Church. He once ended a sermon in St. Mary's by urging upon his audience " the study of Greek literature, which not only elevates above the common herd, but leads not infrequently to positions of considerable emolument."

33 The Divinity School
(*Ackermann's " Oxford "*)

34 Oriel Street and St. Mary's
      Spire

Reformation Oxford
as it was

"FAREWELL, FAREWELL, DEAR OXFORD ; GOD BLESS THEE AND increase thy sons in number, holiness, and virtue." With these words did Queen Elizabeth take leave of the university. She visited it twice, and enjoyed herself enormously on each occasion. She had listened to speeches in Greek and Latin, and had answered them in the same tongues ; she had sat through days of disputation on philosophy and theology ; she had attended indefatigably at banquets, sacraments, and masques. It was a place after her own heart, and she repaid the fulsome compliments of the university with a good share of her royal favour. Her favourite Dudley [1] was made Chancellor, and under his regime the university achieved its formal incorporation and a considerable increase in its powers. But none the less Oxford was rigidly compelled into conformity with the new religious settlement. The Queen's policy was one of compromise and moderation ; but the compromise itself was a Procrustes' bed in which all must lie whether it suited them or not. The visitation of Bishop Horne was not as savage as that of the earlier commissioners ; but it was severe upon the new-glazed windows and new-tuned organs of Mary's time. Oxford was at the outset of Elizabeth's reign the very citadel of the Catholic faith in England. When the Mass became illegal, and later when every member of the university was required to subscribe to the 39 Articles, Oxford began to lose some of its finest men—men such as Edmund Campion of the new College of St. John the Baptist, some of whom departed to the Continent, while others nobly risked their lives to keep their faith alive in England.

Nevertheless, no more colleges were suppressed under Elizabeth, not even the two new Popish colleges of Mary's reign. One new

---

[1] Dudley's wife, Amy Robsart, was buried in St. Mary's Church after her mysterious death at Cumnor, just outside Oxford. His own chaplain preached the sermon, and " tripped once or twice in his speech by recommending to their memories that virtuous lady ' so pitifully murdered ' instead of ' so pitifully slain.' "

35 (*opposite*) : Le Sueur's Statue of Charles I
in the Canterbury Quadrangle of St. John's

college was founded, nominally by Elizabeth herself; this was Jesus College, the particular home of Welsh students, set up in 1571 by Hugh ap Rice upon a site allotted by the Queen.

Oxford's outstanding benefactor in Queen Elizabeth's time was Sir Thomas Bodley, a member of her diplomatic service and formerly a proctor of the university. Bodley was a great lover of books, and in his retirement he took pity upon the desolate condition of Duke Humphrey's Library, whose empty walls, denuded even of their shelving, disgraced the lovely room above the Divinity School. In 1598 he took this work in hand, and four years later the first part of the " Bodleian " Library was opened. Over a century had passed since Duke Humphrey's manuscripts had been first moved in ; the flood of print had begun, in a small way, to inundate the world ; and a single room no longer sufficed to hold the university's books. Bodley therefore planned an extension of his library to the east, over the " Proscholium," the arcade before the entrance of the Divinity School which had since the visitation of 1550 been used as a pig-market. This extension, known as the " Arts End," was completed in 1612. In the next year Bodley died, leaving a large endowment for the purpose of rebuilding all the university schools which stood to the east of his library. Within seven years of his death the whole of the present Schools Quadrangle was finished, and the Schools Tower was fittingly adorned with the effigy of a new monarch flatteringly situated between Religion and Fame.

James I was immensely proud of his own peculiar scholarship, and when he visited Oxford was pleased to crack elaborate scholastic jokes.[1] Two more colleges were founded in his reign. One Nicholas Wadham, a Somersetshire gentleman, bequeathed a sum of money for this purpose. In 1610, his widow founded Wadham College on the site of the former Augustinian friary outside the city walls, and the new buildings were completed three years later. In 1624, one Thomas Tisdall of Abingdon took over a well-known hall in St. Aldate's, and founded it anew as Pembroke College, named after the then Chancellor, Lord Pembroke, who is sometimes identified with the " Mr. W. H." of Shakespeare's sonnets.

The Jacobean period was distinguished in Oxford not only for its new additions to the university, but for an extraordinary activity in the rebuilding of old colleges. No visitor to Oxford can fail to notice that the colleges are mostly built in a style quite peculiar to the place. It is a kind of domesticated Gothic, small in scale and repetitive in detail, extremely well suited to the soft Headington stone and to the purpose of academic lodgings. The

---

[1] James lacked his predecessor's appetite for masque and pageant. " I marvel what they think me to be," he observed on waking from a long sleep during his third Oxford entertainment in three days.

36   The Bodleian : Duke Humphrey's Library (*Ackermann's " Oxford "*)

37   The Bodleian Quad

38   Wadham Chapel (*Ackermann's " Oxford "*)

39   Wadham : the Parks Road Front

perfection of this style is undoubtedly to be seen in Wadham, which was built by masons sent from the Wadham estates in Somerset. As if in admiration of this complete architectural success, half a dozen other colleges set about pulling down their mediæval structures and building afresh. The most characteristic parts of Jesus, Lincoln, and Exeter all belong to this period ; Oriel was entirely rebuilt in exact imitation of the Wadham plan ; a few years later the reconstruction of University College was begun. But the most ambitious undertaking was the new Jacobean work at St. John's, possibly executed by Inigo Jones, but certainly commissioned by the great William Laud.

This man was, so far as Oxford is concerned, the Waynflete or Wolsey of the sixteenth century. His great career began at St. John's, where he was successively scholar, fellow, and President. From Oxford he passed on to great ecclesiastical advancements. Under Charles I he became Archbishop ; but he combined with these duties those of a very active Chancellor of the university. He gave to Oxford the same strict and sometimes galling supervision which he gave to the Church. He promulgated a body of Statutes which were designed not only to bind the university irrevocably to the new church establishment, but also to regulate the conduct of its members in the minutest particulars. They were to " abstain from that absurd and assuming practice of walking publicly in boots " ; to be fined 6s. 8d. for wearing curls or immoderately long hair ; to avoid houses where women of ill or suspected fame were harboured ; to keep away from all houses where wine or tobacco was sold, on pain of being flogged in public if under eighteen years old ; to retire to their colleges before nine ; to abstain from " dibs, dice, and cards," and from hunting wild animals with hounds, ferrets, nets or toils, and from " all parade and display of guns and cross-bows, and from the use of hawks for fowling." They were not to play football, or cudgel-play, particularly in the public streets ; nor to challenge each other to fight ; nor to drive themselves in any vehicles ; nor to carry any offensive or defensive arms, except when setting out upon or returning from a journey to parts remote, or excepting parties who carry bows and arrows for fair amusement's sake. Laud's restrictions did not stop short at the members of his university. He claimed for his proctors a right of search in the townsmen's houses ; he bade all keepers of inns and taverns to repair their back walls and stop up any mazy winding walks in their back areas or gardens ; he provided that all stage-players, rope-dancers or fencers coming to the university for gain's sake should be imprisoned.

Laud was a great churchman, but a busybody of the first order, as these alarming statutes would prove even without his record as a statesman. However, he was a very good friend to his own

college. In his day as President it had consisted of a single quadrangle. It was he who added the " Canterbury " Quadrangle
beyond. In it he adhered to the modest scale of the period, but
he adorned it over and above with an elaborate colonnade, and it
is quite conceivable that for this work he called in the talents of
Inigo Jones, who would have been well known to him at Court.
Proud he was to entertain his King and Queen and young Prince
Rupert in his handsome new library, to join the arms of his see of
Canterbury with the royal arms, to make Rupert a Master of Arts,
and to order Le Sueur to cast fine statues of Charles and Mary to
commemorate the scene.[1]

In another ten years Laud's head was off ; and both Charles
and the Queen had seen far more of Oxford than they wanted to.
But the few peaceful years of the reign gave Oxford another two
of its most charming memorials. One of the minor statesmen of
the day, Lord Danby, converted the old Jews' burial-ground, down
by the Cherwell and facing Magdalen, into a botanical garden,
more properly known as the Physick Garden, since its primary
object was the study and cultivation of herbs. And in the heart
of Oxford a further extension was made to the Bodleian. Bodley
had left it in the shape of a great T : this was converted into the
shape of an H by adding a further wing. The space below it was
used to accommodate the two ruling bodies of the university—
Convocation and Congregation—whose debates were hither transferred from the dark crypt beside St. Mary's Church.

Scarcely was the roof set upon this last building than England
felt the first shocks of a civil war which was to bring Oxford into
special prominence. The strategic importance which the Saxons
had discovered in the place was suddenly revived after centuries
of peace. This importance was not immediately recognised ; for
the first fate of Oxford was to fall unresisting into the hands of a
small Parliamentary force in September 1642. These warriors did
little damage. They stole some plate and burnt some Popish
books ; and then their eyes beheld a horrible spectacle, truly
shocking to good Christians—an image of Christ's mother. This
" very scandalous statue " was not only an outrage to their feel-
ings, but a painful reminder of Archbishop Laud. For the image
had been erected by Laud's own chaplain, who spent a sum of
£230 in building a new porch for St. Mary's. It is a glorious piece
of work, this porch, Oxford's only baroque achievement, and all
the finer from its juxtaposition to the chaste perpendicular of the

[1] Though entertained at St. John's, Charles adhered to royal tradition
by sleeping at Christ Church. Anthony Wood, aged 13, was " conveyed in
a servant's arms to the lodgings of Dr. Thomas Iles, Canon of Christ Church ;
whence being conveyed to the mount in his garden looking into Fish Street
[St. Aldate's] he saw the king, queen and the rest riding down the said street
into Ch. Ch. great quadrangle. . . . Such a glorious train as that was,
he would often talk of when he was a man."

44 Brasenose Front Quad, from a drawing by J. M. W. Turner (1805)

45 Oriel Quad, from a drawing by J. M. W. Turner (1801)

46 Convocation House

47 The Statue of Henrietta
Maria at St. John's

decree of deprivation. His wife and children, after an unsuccessful attempt by the soldiery to " weary them out with noise, rudeness, smell of tobacco, etc.," had to be forcibly removed from the Deanery upon boards, " like pies going to the oven." Many other senior members were evicted by the troops, and Puritan toadies installed in their place.

Yet the flame of learning was not altogether extinguished during the Commonwealth ; and the thanks for this is mostly due to Wadham, the youngest but one of all Oxford's colleges. A certain John Wilkins, a Parliament man of the better sort, became Warden of Wadham in 1648 [1] ; and about the same time young Christopher Wren came up as a gentleman commoner from Westminster. The latter was " a youth of prodigious inventive wit," and he soon outstripped all his instructors. As a gentleman commoner, he sat among the fellows, and soon himself became a Fellow of All Souls. Wilkins had rooms, as had most heads of colleges in those days, over the college gate ; and he allowed the big room with the oriel window to become Wren's " astronomy chamber." Here forgathered Wren's admirers and would-be teachers, to admire the innumerable fruits of his ingenuity. John Wallis and Seth Ward, the Savilian professors of geometry and astronomy ; Lawrence Rooke ; Thomas Sprat, later Bishop of Rochester, scientist and stylist ; William Petty, of universal genius, who founded a great family ; Robert Boyle, " the father of modern science and uncle of the Earl of Cork " : these and others formed a vigorous intellectual circle in Oxford during the Commonwealth. John Evelyn passed through Oxford in 1654, and it was an essential part of his visit to call upon " that miracle of a youth, Mr. Christopher Wren." He " dined at that most obliging and universally curious Dr. Wilkins's at Wadham College." Dr. Wilkins's universal curiosity had led him to invent a transparent bee-hive and a talking statue. " He had, above in his lodgings and gallery, variety of shadows, dials, perspectives . . . a way-wiser, a thermometer, a monstrous magnet, conic and other sections, a balance on a demicircle ; most of them of his own, and that prodigious young scholar Mr. Christopher Wren."

When there came the warm sunshine of the Restoration, this group of faintly grotesque experimentalists was to blossom into the Royal Society ; while Wren was to turn from his astronomy to the highest flights of architecture. All this we owe to Wadham, which excelled so much within fifty years of its foundation.

[1] He did not stay there long. Having obtained a dispensation to marry, contrary to the college statutes, he married Cromwell's own sister, and was rewarded with the Presidency of Trinity College, Cambridge. " From which being ejected at the Restoration, he faced about and by his smooth language, insinuating preaching, flatteries, and I know not what " procured himself the bishopric of Chester.

Reformation Oxford
as it is

I N SETTING OUT TO EXPLORE THE OXFORD OF THESE THREE
reigns, of Elizabeth and James I and Charles I, it would be
impossible to start better than with Wadham College. It was
within this period that the perfect and most natural style of
institutional architecture was evolved. It was at Wadham that
the style achieved its first and most complete success.

Dorothy Wadham, fulfilling like Dervorguilla Balliol the desires
of her dead husband, took over the site of the Augustinian friary
on the road to the Parks. Nothing of the old building was preserved; an entirely new start was made; and the whole college
as it stands was built in the three years from 1610 to 1613. No
other in Oxford presents such an instantly prepossessing façade.
The obscure Somerset stonemasons who built this college attained
a most perfect symmetry and strength without an atom of pre-
tension. Dignity breathes from the tall chimneys, the proud
tower, and the great oriel of Wilkins's astronomy room. Calm and
security are expressed in the long horizontal lines of roof and string-
courses, so artfully pinned down by bay windows at each end, so
skilfully broken to underline the importance of the tower. Here
is perfection in a simple guise.

The quadrangle of Wadham is scarcely less exquisite. Three
sides are squarely, almost smugly residential. The fourth is by
contrast monumental. With twin lanterns and identical windows,
hall and ante-chapel mimic one another: they are divided by one of
those tedious towers of orders, but adorned with the statues of the
good Nicholas and Dorothy Wadham, with James I above them.
Beneath this tower you can enter the hall, which has a highly
characteristic Jacobean screen and a hammerbeam roof of the
contemporary style, less pleasing than that of a century earlier.
Behind the hall is a somewhat desolate cloister, used for the con-
veyance of victuals. The builders of Wadham chapel adhered
to the traditional T-shape; the interior has undergone drastic

44

though unusually skilful alteration. Blore gave the chapel a new roof and reredos, Jackson a new organ-gallery. But it is still remarkable for its windows. Those in the chapel itself preserve a singular purity of perpendicular design, considering that they were put up in the seventeenth century ; and the glass of the east window is the work of a remarkable Dutchman, Bernard van Ling, who, with his brother Abraham, arrived in Oxford about 1620. The van Ling work at Wadham was so greatly admired that the brothers were given half a dozen other commissions, the results of which are to be seen all over Oxford. Certainly if windows must be painted and stained, the work might be done worse than by these gloomy and allegorical Dutchmen.

The perfection of Wadham is also to be seen in its gardens, which are reached by a passage and staircase. From here the chapel looks exactly as Dorothy Wadham's steward intended to make it—the type of a West Country parish church, though without its tower. The garden is large and contains some admirable great trees. The fortunate Warden of Wadham has a still larger garden, though the far end of it was sold not long ago as a site for Rhodes House.

Wadham is a distinguished college in many ways. It has pre-served the West Country tradition handed down by its founders. It was as a son of a West Country parsonage that Christopher Wren came up to Wadham less than thirty years after it opened its doors : the only visible memento of his connection is a clock which he set up above the chapel door. We have seen how Wadham thrived under the Commonwealth ; and from those days it has preserved a staunch Whiggish tradition. At a time when almost all Oxford was Jacobite in sympathy, Wadham honoured the Hanoverians ; and it still possesses, what will not be found in other colleges, portraits of those detested monarchs William III and George I.

An examination of the portraits in the hall will disclose yet a third Wadham tradition. It is a great college for successful lawyers. Lord Birkenhead and Sir John Simon were undergraduates here together.

Returning southwards from Wadham, and running the archi-tectural gauntlet of the new Bodleian, you find the old Bodleian and Bodley's quadrangle just beyond the Clarendon building. The central archway of the Clarendon is aligned with a passage through into the quadrangle, just as the Sheldonian is aligned with the Divinity School next door. Most of Bodley's works were executed in the ten years before and the ten years after Wadham ; but naturally none of them has the same domesticated modesty. The Old Schools Quadrangle itself is somewhat gloomy, from the great height of its side-walls. On its east side is a five-storeyed tower, each storey of which displays a different architectural order. This typical Jacobean conceit, which we have seen already in the

Fellows' Quad at Merton and on a smaller scale at Wadham, was built by Thomas Holt in 1519, completing Bodley's scheme. On the fourth stage are the sculptures which flattered James I; the topmost room was once an observatory. The archway is used only once a year, at the degree-giving ceremony; it has a fine original pair of doors on the street side, bearing the arms of all the colleges down to Wadham.

Looking around the quadrangle, you will see that every little door has a Latin name above it, denoting this or that faculty as "Schola medicinæ" or "Schola naturalis philosophiæ." These are mere sentimental reminders of the original use of the buildings. This was at first the centre of all teaching; but by degrees the university's monstrous collection of books has ousted everything else. Floor by floor the books have crept round and round. As late as the 1880's some examinations continued to be held here; but now the whole place is solid with books. The nucleus of the entire library is on the west side of the quadrangle. The wall which faces the tower is elaborately stone-panelled, and contains a wide seven-light window. This window lights the ancient library, to which access is by a stairway through a small door in the left-hand corner.

The ancient part of Bodley's library grew in the shape of an H. The visitor may only enter the first wing of the H, wherein the books are arranged *along* the walls, with a gallery. This is the "Arts End," built in 1612. The corresponding wing is the "Selden End," built in 1634-40.[1] The long room which connects the two is Duke Humphrey's Library, finished in 1480, denuded of books in 1550, and reopened by Bodley in 1602. Here the books are arranged in bays, as was the universal fashion until the Arts End was built. Bodley's arms alternate with those of the university in the painted ceiling. This, which must be one of the loveliest rooms in all the world, is reserved for students only, though few undergraduates pursue any studies in it.

A little farther up the stairway by which you entered, you come to a sort of public showroom run in connection with the Bodleian as a bait to draw visitors away from the interesting parts. Here is to be seen a very mixed collection of objects—a quantity of Napoleon's furniture bequeathed by Lord Curzon, an aspidistra, a letter in the hand of King George V, a chair made from the timbers of Drake's ship, a portrait of Cromwell, and so forth. More interesting are the special displays of books and manuscripts arranged here from time to time.

[1] When Selden's books were brought to Oxford, Anthony Wood " laboured several weeks with Mr. Thomas Barlow and others in sorting them, carrying them up stairs, and placing them. In opening some of the books they found several pairs of spectacles which Mr. Selden had put in and forgotten to take out, and Mr. Thomas Barlow gave A. W. a pair which he kept in memory of Selden to his last day."

BIBLIOTHECA PUBLICA BODLEIANA & SCHOLÆ *sive* AUDITORIA ARTIUM LIBERALIUM *ut ad Austrum Spectantur.*

A Scholæ publicæ
B Bibliotheca prid Bodleiana
C Schola Theologiæ
D Domus Convocationis
E Portico's sive ambulacra
F ... plat... ... ...
G G ... idos... ...

Insignia Re: Bodleii.

Insignia Univ: Oxon.

Scale of feete

D. Loggan delin et sculp cum privil S R M.

48 The Bodleian : from Loggan's *Oxonia Illustrata* (1675)

49   Christ Church : fro

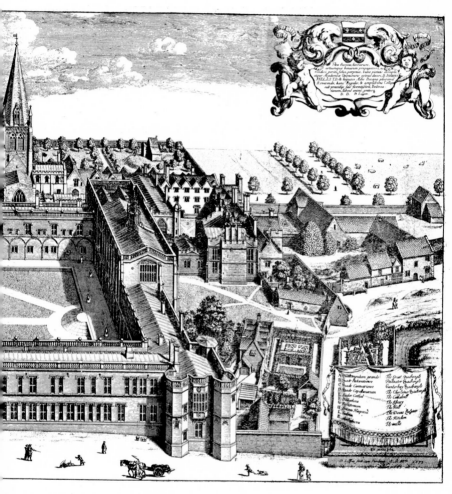

Oxonia Illustrata (1675)

50   Wadham : from Loggan's *Oxonia Illustrata* (1675)

Sir Thomas Bodley made an arrangement with the Stationers' Company that his library should receive a free copy of every book printed by members of that company. Various Copyright Acts have confirmed this privilege, so that now the library receives a copy of every book printed in England, however trivial or worthless it may be. Hundreds of books are added daily; an army of employees is required to handle them; the catalogue alone occupies an entire wing—and not one book in a thousand ever leaves its shelf again.

This flood of printed matter has engulfed not only the Old Schools, but the Radcliffe Camera as well. Beneath the soil of Radcliffe Square a great underground store has been excavated. By decentralisation, whole sections of the library have been transferred to other institutions. But still the problem arises ever anew, how to find room for all this trash. A million pounds is now being spent upon the solution of it, in a manner which Oxford will have reason to repent.

If you return to Old Schools Quadrangle, and enter the arch beneath Bodley's wide window, you are in the Proscholium or one-time pig-market. Before entering the Divinity School by the door in front of you, it is worth while to notice the shoddy style of the stone vaulting in this arcade; for by contrast the roof of the Divinity School itself is a miracle of architecture. All the Gothic masonry in England can show nothing finer than the marvellous elaboration of these low arches with their enormous pendants, and the rich carvings at the intersections of every rib. This work, together with the chapel of King's at Cambridge, displays the very latest fruition of the perpendicular style about the middle of the fifteenth century.

When the commissioners of Edward VI removed Duke Humphrey's books from the room above, they also destroyed the stained glass of the Divinity School below. The purity of style is much enhanced by the plain glass. Less congruous features of the room are the wooden platform and classical balustrades at the west end and a mock-Gothic doorway in the north wall. These are the work of Sir Christopher Wren, and in the latter he has used the same ogee-shaped canopy as at Tom Tower.

At the far end of the Divinity School is the entrance to the Convocation House, a miniature Parliament where the law-making bodies of the university have met since 1640. The detail of this room is vastly inferior to that of the Divinity School: indeed, a space of a hundred and sixty years divides the two.

Opening in turn from the Convocation House is a small Robing Room, of some interest because it is fitted up as a miniature Court. This is where the heads of colleges struggle into their gowns; it is also the room where the Vice-Chancellor dispenses justice. He can not only claim to try any local suit in which a member of the

47

university is sued by a stranger[1] : but he can try the members them-selves on any charge but treason, felony or mayhem. However, the Court sits so rarely that the scandal is more potential than real.

The whole of this building is so drenched in beauty and antiquity that mere dates and episodes add little to its fascination. It should, however, be recorded that a House of Commons has twice met within its walls. In 1681, when Charles II exercised an undoubted but unpopular right to assemble Parliament in Oxford, the Con-vocation House was allotted to the Commons, who arrived in a mood of truculent assurance and were sent off a few days later having had their legs properly pulled for them. Their fathers in 1644 had met in the Divinity School in a very different mood, when Charles I gathered round him the loyal and devoted minority of the Commons. And just a century before that again these same walls had heard the frantic exculpations of Latimer, Ridley, and Cranmer, as they struggled in the net of Cardinal Pole. So does each high tide of national history leave its faint tidemark on Oxford's walls.

Various influences were united to create in the reign of James I a great activity in expansion and rebuilding at Oxford. The king was a friend to learning, while the fires of Smithfield were burnt down to a mere ember. Confidence returned too soon. It seems also that the design of Wadham had aroused immediate admira-tion ; and other colleges, still cramped in mediæval discomfort, wished to be as beautifully housed. The Wadham influence is very clearly to be seen in many places ; while the plan of Oriel, whose rebuilding began in 1619, was at first an almost literal copy.

From the Bodleian, Oriel is reached past St. Mary's Church and down Oriel Street, a narrow way which contains the most expensive lodgings in Oxford. The whole east wall is Oriel's boundary, and the gate is at the bottom. Nobody knows for certain the derivation of the name Oriel.

In the first quadrangle the only important variant on the Wadham design is the addition of very unattractive gables of alternating patterns. Opposite the entrance are two awkward statues like weathercocks and an awkward portico, whose inscrip-tion " Regnante Carolo " marks the date of the completion of the quad. Hall and ante-chapel balance each other, with twin lanterns ; but in this case the relative positions are reversed. The chapel, set strangely askew, is small and dull, and much restored by Sir T. G. Jackson. The hall is inaccessible and dull.

---

[1] This right was asserted in a libel action in 1886, and upheld by the Lord Chief Justice. Anthony Wood attended at the Apoditerium in 1693 as defendant in an action brought by the second Earl of Clarendon on account of a libel he had published on the first Earl. Dean Aldrich as Vice-Chancellor heard the suit. Wood was fined, and his book was ordered to be burnt in the theatre yard.

51   University College from the High

52   Lincoln, from a drawing by F. Mackenzie (1823)

53   St. John's : the Inner Quad

54   St. John's : the Garden Front

Oriel began to extend northwards after another hundred years. In the 1720's a new open quad was formed to the north, and the old style was closely followed in the two new wings. In 1788 this second quad was adorned by a splendid library by Wyatt in a severe Ionic style. The actual library, as so often, is on the upper floor ; beneath it is one of the few good common rooms in Oxford. Such rooms are never public and seldom worth inspection : but Oriel common room is distinguished not only in design, but by its associations. In the middle of the nineteenth century it was the intellectual centre of Oxford. Both the Arnolds, Keble, Pusey, Newman, Clough, and R. H. Froude were among the fellows of Oriel. It was the home of the Oxford Movement, and all good Anglicans should revere its shrine.

Between Wyatt's library and the High Street was the site of St. Mary Hall, one of the four ancient halls which survived into the last century. It had flourished as a separate dependency of Oriel ever since 1333, and the Royal Commissioners proposed that Oriel should annex it. At the moment when this fusion was about to take place there died a former undergraduate, the magnificent Cecil Rhodes. He left his old college £100,000, with which they erected one of Oxford's worst buildings on their newly acquired territory. By two passages, one on either side of the library, you can reach what was the quadrangle of St. Mary Hall. The three old sides are charming : but the north side is a specimen of Mr. Basil Champneys at his most disgusting. This edifice was completed in 1911 ; from the even less attractive front which it presents to the High Street, statues of Rhodes, Edward VII, and George V compete for notice with the saints and angels of St. Mary's.

The next college to follow Oriel's lead in making a clean sweep of its old buildings was University College, its neighbour to the east. University College, or " Univ." as it is more concisely called, has always occupied its present position on the south side of the High Street, to which it presents a long and slightly crooked frontage in two halves, balanced even to having a pair of gate towers. The entrance is by the first of these, if you are going down the High Street—the second, if you come up by Logic Lane.

University College has already been conceded the first place in order of antiquity ; but not content with this distinction, the college has long claimed an even remoter origin, and has honoured as its founder none other than Alfred the Great. This claim apparently was based upon some title-deed or other document, which at some distant period was brought into being by the college authorities in order to clinch a lawsuit. The same recital even claimed that the Venerable Bede, who died nearly two centuries before Alfred, had been a fellow of the college. The legend thus dishonestly fathered has survived to a quite recent time. In 1872

9

the fellows solemnly celebrated their thousandth anniversary, and were quite pained when the Regius Professor of History sent them a burnt cake as his contribution to the festivities.

This Alfred-the-Great delusion was a foible long shared by the whole university. Anthony Wood, a quite serious antiquary of the seventeenth century, devotes the better part of a quarto volume to an entirely imaginary chronicle of Oxford's early days. He tells us that Alfred's son Edward was educated at Oxford and "applied himself to learning"; that in turn he sent his son Ailfward, who "became eminently learned"; that another son Ethelstan was "thought by several to have been educated in the Schools at Oxford"; and so forth. All this is pure imagination.[1] The actual buildings of University College are just three centuries old. The main quadrangle was begun in 1634, delayed by the wars, and finished forty years later. Here, as at Oriel, the effect of the regular close-set windows is marred by the crowding together of over-elaborate gables. On the south side, which comprises the hall and chapel, these gables were removed in 1800 and replaced by battlements and pinnacles. The hall is an unattractive room, having been enlarged out of all proportion by two extra bays on the west. It has a remarkable but ugly hammerbeam roof, and contains a good portrait of William Windham by Lawrence. The chapel has been mutilated by Sir George Gilbert Scott; but it retains its handsome marble floor, an excellent Corinthian screen, and some vigorous contemporary stained glass by the younger van Ling brother, Abraham. There is a fine Flaxman monument in the ante-chapel. Beyond the hall is a Gothic library by Scott.

The second quad, reached by a passage on the east side, is a successful fake, having been built in imitation of the other in the years 1716–19, long after the style was dead. It constitutes one of the countless benefactions of Dr. Radcliffe. The little-used gateway is notable for an elaborate fan-vault. On the inner side of the tower is a very good statue of the lavish Doctor; on the outer side is Queen Mary, consort of William III. The corresponding statues on the older tower are Queen Anne and James II. This latter is worth observing as one of the only two statues extant of England's catholic king; it was erected by Obadiah Walker,[2] a Catholic Master of Univ. who lost his office when James fell off his throne.

If you follow a corridor in the north-west corner of the principal quad, you will come upon a still more noteworthy piece of statuary.

---

[1] Some eighteenth-century antiquaries maintained that King Alfred "revived" an already ancient university. One of them published a history of the university "to the death of William the Conqueror."

[2] "Old Obadiah," chanted the undergraduates,
"Sings Ave Maria;
So do not I—ah."

In a sunk well beneath a once starry dome lies the effigy of Percy Bysshe Shelley, laid out naked and drowned like a turbot on a slab. This work is by Onslow Ford, and its setting by Basil Champneys, and it was set up in 1893. The undergraduate thus fulsomely honoured in his death received short shrift from the college authorities in his lifetime. He would appear to have been a singularly tiresome youth. After a few terms of residence he wrote a pamphlet on "The Necessity of Atheism"; he distributed copies of it to all the heads of houses, and then pedantically refused to admit it as his own; whereupon he was very rightly sent down in a state of puerile excitement.[1]

The remaining buildings of Univ. are a west wing on the High Street by Sir Charles Barry, a Master's house by Bodley, and an extension on the far side of Logic Lane by H. W. Moore.

Radcliffe Square, the central point of the university, lies between the Old Schools and St. Mary's. It takes its name from this same Dr. Radcliffe who did so well by University College. All Souls takes up its east side. Brasenose College, or "B.N.C.," stands on the west, and its old gate is under the shadow of the Radcliffe Camera.

It is hard to assign a period to Brasenose. It was founded in 1509, and the present front quadrangle was finished about 1516; but by far the most noticeable feature of this quad is an array of large and elaborate dormers added in the time of James I. The tower itself, first dwindled in proportion by this extra storey and then overwhelmed by the vast dome of the Radcliffe Camera, is a Victorian restoration, well executed by a Mr. Buckler. The hall on the south front has had a more recent oriel bay added to it : above the high table is the brazen nose itself, brought back from Stamford after 557 years. The former chapel in this first quad became long since a senior common room.

Brasenose had a Dr. Radcliffe of its own, like his namesake a great benefactor. He it was who built the big dormers, and dying in 1648, left money for a new chapel. This was built on a new site to the south of the old quad, in the years from 1656 to 1666, together with a new cloister and library. These Commonwealth buildings, belonging to a period when scarcely any building was done in England, are of a strange transitional style. Externally the chapel is rather pleasing; inside, it has a most remarkable roof which compromises between the hammerbeam and the fan-vault, though the latter is only a fake of lath and plaster.

There have been many bold schemes for the rebuilding of Brasenose. Hawksmoor contrived a plan about 1723 in the

[1] A few years earlier, Walter Savage Landor was sent down from Trinity in very similar circumstances. He had fired a gun from his window, and had refused with equal childishness to admit the offence, although the evidence against him was plain enough.

manner of Queen's, if possible more ponderous still; it is to be seen in a contemporary book called *Oxonia Depicta*. A century later Sir John Soane, whose genius is unrepresented in Oxford, drew up another comprehensive plan, drawings of which are in the library. Wyatt remodelled the library itself to some extent; but the great expansion of Brasenose took place in an unfortunate architectural period. Like both Oriel and Queen's, the college finally achieved a frontage on the High Street, where it has a new gateway. The architect for the southern quadrangle was Sir T. G. Jackson, who also made many alterations in the chapel. Jackson was a deeply learned man, and he enjoyed a great renown; but his work is wholly uninspired. The best one can say for him is that he was a better architect than Mr. Basil Champneys.

B.N.C. is renowned among all other colleges for " heartiness." Its undergraduates are as broad and heavy as prize cattle, and their speech is of " toggers " and " heats " : it is said that scholarships are awarded to likely athletes. George Washington's great-grandfather was a member of the college in 1619. When he left he owed the buttery 17*s.* 10*d.* This obligation was discharged in 1924 by some American visitors.

Before passing on to St. John's and its Laudian splendours, there are three lesser colleges to be included—optionally, as it were—in a survey of the period. Two of them, Jesus and Lincoln, stand just at the back of Brasenose, in the Turl; the third, Pembroke, is far away in St. Aldate's, opposite the House. None of the three calls for very much attention except from the most leisured visitor.

The Turl is the least attractive of the old parts of Oxford. Narrow and confined, it runs from Broad Street opposite Trinity to High Street by the Mitre, between the high walls of unattractive colleges. Jesus stands on the right as you go south. As its founder intended, it is still a hotbed of Welshmen, and the names at the foot of every staircase consist predominantly of Joneses and Evanses. The present frontage dates from 1856, when the conscientious Buckler made it Gothic : before that, for just a century it had been a ponderous classical block. The two small quadrangles consist of old buildings gothicised in the time of the Regency. The chapel was finished in 1621, but has been wholly ruined by George Edmund Street. The hall is contemporary, and contains a van Dyck portrait of Charles I, a portrait of Elizabeth by a nameless artist, and a Lawrence portrait of John Nash. Jesus is a small college, and its members play little part in the life of the university.

On the other side of the Turl, a little farther down, is Lincoln, which was founded in 1427. The first quad, the northernmost of the two, belongs to that period ; so does the tiny hall, the interior of which has been classicised. In the time of James I the college expanded to double its size; and the southern quadrangle was built between 1610 and 1631. The chapel in this quad is a good example of its kind. The windows are contemporary; but the fine cedar woodwork was installed in 1686. John Wesley was a fellow of Lincoln for nine years before his excursion to Georgia, and the chapel contains a pulpit from which he used to preach. The front of the college was gothicised in 1819, at the same time as the quadrangles of Jesus. The work was so well done that Pugin himself made drawings of it as an original Gothic exemplar. In 1930 a Rectors' House was built in the Turl, to the south of the college; it will be a handsome work when the stone has weathered.

In 1624, Broadgates Hall became Pembroke College. The new foundation took over the older buildings, which were perched upon the city wall, just by the south gate. At intervals between 1670 and 1694 the quadrangle was rebuilt in a vaguely Carolean style. In the nineteenth century the north front was badly gothicised, and a new wing added, the effect of which was to cramp the entrance-tower into an undignified corner. The hall is also Victorian. For a century the college had no chapel, and its devotions were conducted in the south aisle of the depressing church of St. Aldate outside the gate. The present chapel was built in 1728–32. The plain classical exterior is smothered in creeper : the interior is an unpleasant restoration by Kempe, rendered worse by stained glass. The wall of the garden beyond the chapel is part of the old city wall. Pembroke's greatest fame rests upon the fourteen months' residence of Samuel Johnson. There is said to be a Reynolds portrait of him in the senior common room. His rooms were on the second floor over the gate.

St. John's is a college that every visitor should see. It stands in St. Giles's, more usually known as the Giler, behind a screen of ancient elms. Several colleges formerly had such terraces before their gates, notably Balliol; but St. John's alone has kept it.

We have seen how St. John's was founded in 1555 by Sir Thomas White; but most of the first quadrangle is older than that, for White was able to buy the deserted buildings of St. Bernard's College, which was founded as early as 1436 by Archbishop Chichele of All Souls, and had been suppressed at the Reformation. The tower over the entrance gate dates from 1437 ; it was one of the few buildings in Oxford to be hit during the siege of 1646. The south and west sides of the first quadrangle are very old except for their dormer windows. The north side comprises the chapel and hall, built between 1500 and 1530. They both underwent much alteration in the eighteenth century, since when the chapel has endured successive redecorations at the hands of both Blore and Kempe, so that there is little left to see.

Towards the end of the sixteenth century the east side of this quadrangle was completed, and a start was made upon a new library which is now part of the further quadrangle. It was in this modest form that Edmund Campion knew his college. He was a fellow of St. John's from 1557 to 1569; his learning and eloquence drew worship from his listeners; he was chosen to deliver a "rather patronising" oration at the funeral of Sir Thomas White.

Eight years after the martyrdom of Campion, William Laud received his scholarship at St. John's. In 1593 he became a fellow, in 1611 President of the college. In 1631, when he was Chancellor of the University and Bishop of London, he began the second quadrangle; in 1636, as Archbishop of Canterbury, he finished it off with all the pomp and gaiety of a royal visit. The whole work, in style and spirit, belongs entirely to the reign of Charles I. The north and south ranges are unpretentious, save for the magnificent lead rainwater-heads adorned with royal and archiepiscopal arms. The ranges to east and west are more ceremonial. Their ornate colonnades, in the purest spirit of the Italian Renaissance, are quite possibly the work of Inigo Jones; at all events, they are wholly unlike any other work in Oxford. The archways at either end are adorned with curious fan-vaults, and surmounted by splendid bronze statues of Charles and his queen by Le Sueur, framed in excellent baroque surrounds. These statues were put up for sale during the Commonwealth; but some good loyalist preserved them for our delectation.

The upper storey of the south and east ranges contains the Laudian library, a beautiful room entirely ruined by Blore. Laud himself was buried in the chapel of St. John's after his execution. There, also, lies his successor Juxon, who should be remembered. Juxon was a scholar of the Merchant Taylors' School in London. Owing to the fact that Sir Thomas White was a Merchant Taylor, a strong link was forged between the college and that famous school, a connection which still subsists. Juxon was Laud's pupil and protégé; he became vicar of the neighbouring church of St. Giles, which belongs to the college; he succeeded Laud both as President and as Bishop of London; he attained high Government offices; and he it was who received the last words of Charles I on the scaffold, and who buried his king. During the Commonwealth he lived in the country, and kept a pack of hounds; he was once reprimanded for allowing them to run through Chipping Campden churchyard. On the Restoration, he was at once appointed Archbishop of Canterbury. Three years later he died, and was buried in the chapel of St. John's, to which he bequeathed a large benefaction.

Beyond the "Canterbury" Quadrangle you gain the gardens of St. John's, which are large and very famous for their beauty. The vast lawn, with its undulating fringe of trees, is so skilfully laid out that the plan has variously been ascribed to Repton, to Capability Brown, and to both of them. The lawn is sometimes used for archery contests. There is a remarkable rockery in the north-west corner. From the lawn, you get a superlative view of the east front of Laud's library wing. With its stately gables and its five great oriels, this façade is as entirely perfect as that of Wadham.

St. John's was much enlarged by Sir George Gilbert Scott in 1881. He built a north wing in continuation of the street front, which is not unsuccessful. Still farther to the north stood Campion Hall, until its migration a few years ago. This Jesuit training college rented its premises from Campion's old college, and carried on his work and his ideals within a hundred yards of the place where they had taken shape.

Classical Oxford
as it was

I N THE OXFORD OF THE RESTORATION PERIOD THERE LIVED AN obscure and solitary antiquarian called Anthony Wood. He was a Master of Arts, and a member of Merton College; and he liked to write his name " à Wood." His contemporaries ignored the existence of this individual; but it is mostly through his writings that their memory has survived. He set himself to write the Annals of the University. By adopting the existing legends on the origins of Oxford he added a good two centuries to the length of its life; but in all other respects his Annals are admirable. Guided by written records, of which he had immense knowledge, Wood pieced together a chronicle of the Middle Ages, on which all later writers have drawn. In his second volume he came to his own times; and the closer they approached the sphere of Wood's own knowledge, the spicier the Annals became. In a final work, called the *Life and Times of Anthony à Wood*, all pretence of history is dropped, and the author resorts to straight and vigorous gossip.

Wood's point of view was that of a disappointed man. He was " utterly unknown to the generality of Scholars " and " by the vulgar at least taken to be a *Rom. Cath.*" For his part, he was persuaded that Oxford was not what it had been. As for the scholars, " their aim is to live like gentlemen, to keep dogs and horses, to turn their studies and coalholes into places to receive bottles, to swash it in apparell, to wear long periwigs, etc.; and the theologists to ride abroad in grey coats with swords by their sides." The age, he complains, is " given over to all vice—whores and harlots, pimps and panders, bawds and buffoons, lechery and treachery, atheists and papists, rogues and rascalls, playmakers and stageplayers, officers debauched and corrupters—aggravated and promoted by presbytery." Later, it is " bawdy houses and light huswifes giving divers young men the pox so that that disease is very common among them and some obscure pocky doctors obtain a living by it "; and " brandy much drank since

55 The Radcliffe Camera

56 Queen's Chapel (*Ackermann's* " *Oxford* ")

this war began with the Dutch." The poor, bitter, dim little man showed little discrimination in his criticisms. At one time he curses the " multitudes of ale-houses " ; a few pages on he states that " the decay of study, and consequently of learning, are coffee-houses, to which most scholars retire and spend much of the day in speaking vily of their superiors." Coffee, he records, was introduced to Oxford in 1650 by Jacob, a Jew; it was specially favoured by the self-esteemed " virtuosi or wits " of All Souls.

Wood was particularly happy when he could bring home some scandal against an individual member of the university. " Mr. R. B., a chaplain of Christ Church, one much given to the flesh and a great lover of Eliz the wife of Funker "—so starts a long and scurrilous tale of mistaken identity.[1] Exeter College, he reports in 1655, is " now much debauched by a drunken Governor," and is a " rude and uncivil house " : the Rector is a good scholar but " much given to bibbing." A newly elected Master of Balliol is described as having " spent most of his time in bibbing and smoking, and nothing of a gent. to carry him off." At St. John's, " a most debauched college," are four undergraduates known to be atheists, who " come drunk into chapel and vomit into their hats or caps there. . . . The next college that wants a thorough reformation is New College, much given to drinking and gaming, and vain brutish pleasure. They degenerate in learning." A would-be Warden of Wood's own college is described as " the very lol-poop of the University, a most lascivious person, a great haunter of women's company and a common fornicator " : Merton College had better be " dissolved again, rather than Tom Clayton should be warden thereof." Yet Warden he became, this " common subject of every lampoon."

Wood's picture of the depravity of Oxford is not altogether imaginary. So far as drink is concerned, this is a reproach that has been made in every age. Dudley Earl of Leicester, as Chancellor, had rebuked the scholars in 1582 for a propensity to " jelt in the Stretes and to tipple in Tavernes." A contemporary of Wood's records in 1674 tells how a student of Christ Church was found dead of drink with a brandy bottle in one hand and the cork in the other. Thirty years later a gentleman commoner at Magdalen died of a surfeit of brandy. In every century there have been strange tales of senior fellows found in compromising situations, and chaplains taken unawares. That Oxford suffered in its moral standards by the Civil Wars cannot be doubted. For

[1] Years later this same gentleman reappears. " Richard Berry being either besotted with drink or with love of Bess Faukner, did stab himself with a knife in the breast and belly several times on the 7 of June about 6 in the morning in his chamber in the Chaplains' Quadrangle at Christ Church." After this episode he was " not permitted to keep his place," but was " sent into Ireland " and " got into some cathedral. This Richard Berry was a fiddler's son of Burford."

10

three years it had harboured a court of highly sophisticated persons. Poor Dr. Kettell, the President of Trinity, had been hurried into his grave by the profligacy of the fine ladies who trespassed in his college and garden. Standards were relaxed, as they were after the Great War. Puritanism stood at a heavy discount, and no wonder. But the age of Wren was emphatically not an age of decadence.

In 1660, when all England was rejoicing at the Restoration, Edward Hyde, Earl of Clarendon, became Chancellor of Oxford. This appointment began a period of high favour for the loyal university. In 1663, Charles II paid a state visit of a week with his Queen, the Duke of York, and Lady Castlemaine.[1] Two years later he returned again to sojourn at Christ Church while London lay beneath the plague. This time he brought the Queen, Lady Castlemaine, and the lovely Miss Stuart. The Duke of Monmouth lodged at Corpus; the Spanish ambassador at New College, and the French ambassador at Magdalen; in Merton, Lady Castlemaine gave birth to a future Duke of Northumberland [2]; while an obstructive Parliament debated in the Convocation House.

Fifteen years later, when Charles was fighting an unscrupulous enemy for the preservation of his throne, he bethought himself again of Oxford and its unwavering loyalty. The situation which faced him was much the same as that which his father had mishandled by his policy of appeasement. Treason and fanaticism had claimed victims enough in the previous three years; Charles saw that he must bring off something in the nature of a *coup d'état* if Monmouth was to be outwitted; but the Earl of Shaftesbury's private army made it impossible to carry off such a stroke in London. Therefore in January 1681 he summoned a Parliament to meet in Oxford. There were good precedents for such a measure; and it was just possible for him to ignore the outcry that it caused. So in March the King arrived at Christ Church; and his angry opponents were obliged to follow him, trooping in one by one over Magdalen Bridge with whatever gangs of ruffians they could get to tramp the sixty miles. Here Charles was safe.[3] He had negotiated with the King of France a contract which should make him free from the insane demands of his Whig parliaments; in Oxford he was not to be intimidated into giving away the succession to his throne or the lives of his supporters.

[1] " 1663, 28 Sept., the king touched divers score of people affected with the king's evil in the choir of Ch. Ch. after that morning service was done. . . . The cage and pillory was taken down to make room for the King's passage in North Gate Street."
[2] " Libel on the Countess of Castlemaine's door in Merton College :
' Hanc Cæsare pressam a fluctu defendit onus.' "
[3] " The general cry was ' long live King Charles,' and many drawing up to the very coach window cried ' Let the king live, and the devil hang up all roundheads '; at which his majesty smiled and seemed well pleased."

J. Farington R.A. del.ᵗ   View in BROAD-STREET in Oxford.   Abridgment Gall.⁴ Hal Oil Aquafort.   I.C. Stadler Sculp.ᵗ

Pub. June 1 1796 by J.& J. Boydell.

57   The Broad in 1796 : from Boydell's *History of the River Thames*

The Commons met in the Convocation House, and on March 28th they were to debate once more the exclusion of the Duke of York. The Lords sat in the Geometry School, which was in the Old Schools Tower, just across the quadrangle. There Charles betook himself in ordinary clothes, as if to indulge his common amusement of listening to the debate. His robes of State, needed for a dissolution, followed in a sedan chair. In secrecy, he put them on, faced the Lords, and sent across to summon the Commons. This message was taken by the Whigs for a sign of immediate surrender. Through the Divinity School they came, in highest spirits, across the quadrangle, and singly up a spiral stairway in Bodley's tower. When they had crowded in, to hear as they supposed the King's submission, he coolly dissolved the Parliament and sent his enemies about their business. Within a few hours he was at Windsor. His victory was complete. Taken by surprise and robbed of their unconstitutional support, the Whigs made haste to shake off the dust of the loyal city, and fled each man to the safest refuge he could find.

Oxford was true to Charles II because Charles was true to the Church, outwardly at least. When the university differed from his brother James, it showed as little fear or servility as the most arrogant Whig could desire. Upon James's accession, many secret Catholics avowed their faith ; and among these was Obadiah Walker, the ancient Master of University College. The university was alarmed when Walker opened a Catholic chapel in his college ; it was staggered when another Catholic was made Dean of Christ Church in succession to Dr. Fell. Yet this office was in the gift of the Crown, whereas the Presidency of Magdalen was not. In 1686 the latter became vacant. What followed thereafter is text-book history. James " beat his head against the walls of Magdalen," trying to push in a disreputable Catholic of his own choice. It was the beginning of the end for him.

All these vicissitudes showed that Oxford had become entirely wedded to the reformed established Church. The university was the great mother of loyal churchmen ; and here at least, the establishment was safe from the attacks of Papist and Presbyterian alike. Translated into politics, this allegiance meant Toryism ; and Oxford's Toryism incurred the suspicious enmity of William III, who visited the university only to insult it. So doubtful did he feel, or affect to feel, as to the loyalty of Oxford that he declined to eat a banquet that had been prepared for him.[1]

---

[1] " The University was at great charge in providing a banquet for the king ; but the king would not eat anything, but went out ; and some rabble and townsmen that had got in seized upon the banquet in the face of the whole University." On the occasion of James II's visit to Oxford to rebuke the fellows of Magdalen, he had been given a banquet in the Selden End of the Bodleian. This was a different kind of failure, as " none did eat but he, for he spake to nobody to eat," despite the presence of 20 large dishes of sweetmeats,

" The Bear," they called him in London for his hateful manners ; it took him less than an hour to write himself down at Oxford as something worse than a bear.

Queen Anne, throughout her life, treasured nothing above her devotion to the Church of England. Her relations with Oxford were cordial and lasting. She was warmly welcomed in the year of her accession, on her way to Bath. During her reign, two singular men adorned the high table at Magdalen. One was Addison, a moderate Whig ; the other was Dr. Sacheverell, the oleaginous High Churchman whose impeachment proved the undoing of the Whigs. The extreme Tory Atterbury was Dean of Christ Church for a while.

Oxford was lukewarm towards the Protestant Succession. Wadham might cherish its portraits of William and of George I ; but there were many non-jurors among the Oxford clergy to whom the Hanoverians were usurpers ; and nowhere was there much enthusiasm for their cause. There were even certain active demonstrations of disloyalty to the new regime. A " Constitution Club " organised by the Whig minority attempted to combat the " vast torrent of treason which overflowed the University " by celebrating the new King's birthday on May 28th, and by burning Dr. Sacheverell in effigy. Their meetings at the King's Head were broken up by riotous Tories. The following day, May 29th, being the anniversary of the Restoration, afforded to the Tories an opportunity to stage a much more successful demonstration by way of rejoinder. June 10th, moreover, was the Pretender's birthday ; so in that age of bonfires this was an anxious fortnight. The worst that happened was an attempt to shoot a Jacobite student from the windows of Oriel. The authorities visited all these disturbances with strict Tory partiality. It was reputed that the proctors kept a " black book " of the names of all " whigs, constitutioners, and bangorians." They suspended the steward of the Constitution Club for two years from taking his degree as a punishment for having compelled one of the proctors to drink the health of King George I.

Oxford's doubtful allegiance was the cause of two celebrated epigrams. The authorities in London took a sufficiently grave view of the recurrent Jacobite riots to dispatch some soldiery to Oxford. The fervent loyalty of low-church Cambridge shone so brightly by contrast in the eyes of the King that he made a handsome gift of books to that less independent university. On this an Oxford wit wrote these lines :

> The King, observing with judicious eyes
> The state of both his Universities,

" piled high like so many ricks of hay," 24 plates of wet sweetmeats, 28 large dishes of cold fish and flesh, 3 hot dishes, and 36 plates of salads. At Carfax, " the conduit ran claret for the vulgar, which was conveyed up there in vessels."

58, 59 Scenes of Oxford Life, *ca.* 1815, from drawings by Thomas Rowlandson

60 " A Varsity Trick—Smuggling In," from a drawing by Thomas
Rowlandson

> To Oxford sent a troop of horse, for why ?
> That learned body wanted loyalty :
> To Cambridge books he sent, as well discerning
> How much that loyal body wanted learning.

This was immediately answered by a Cambridge man :

> The King to Oxford sent a troop of horse,
> For Tories own no argument but force :
> With equal skill to Cambridge books he sent,
> For Whigs admit no force but argument.

The latter of these epigrams is not merely neat : it contains two of the soundest generalisations ever made upon English politics.

The mantle of Anthony Wood fell in Hanoverian times upon another antiquary, equally bitter and equally observant. Thomas Hearne was intended by nature for a librarian ; the Bodleian was his paradise : but he could not take an oath of loyalty to the new King, and all his hopes of useful employment were frustrated. Like Wood, when he was not poring over the records of other ages, he was recording the faults and vices of his own. His point of view was that of the thorough-paced Jacobite. To him the reigning King was and remained " the Duke of Brunswick." In his view nothing good could come out of Germany. Even when Handel himself, the darling of the Court, the rage of London, came to give concerts in the Sheldonian, poor Hearne could only grumble about " one Handel a foreigner," and his " lousy crew of foreign fiddlers," having the use of the theatre.

Hearne is for ever on about the decay of learning, and the desuetude of old manners and observances. The strange thing is that his criticisms are largely corroborated by a writer whose point of view was diametrically opposed to his own. Nicholas Amhurst was a young and outspoken Whig. Possibly because of his political views, he was expelled from Oxford in 1719 ; and he took his revenge by issuing a periodical in which the university was systematically attacked and satirised. He called his paper *Terræ Filius*, which was the name applied to a participant in the annual Encænia, whose part it was to enliven and sometimes to disgrace the solemnity by much licensed buffoonery and ribaldry. The name was well chosen. If *Terræ Filius* is to be believed, Oxford in the 1720's was a sewer of all imaginable vice and corruption.[1] Every don was carrying on an open liaison with his bedmaker ; every undergraduate had his particular " toast " among the loose women with whom the town abounded. Magdalen Grove and Merton gardens were the particular centres of

---

[1] For example, " I have known a profligate debauchee chosen professor of moral philosophy ; and a fellow, who never looked upon the stars soberly in his life, professor of astronomy ; we have had history professors, who have never read anything to qualify them for it, but Tom Thumb, Jack the giant-killer, and such-like valuable records."

dalliance and picking-up. Learning counted for nothing; holy orders were meaningless. Drink, wenching, and disloyalty were the three obsessions of the Oxford man. Extravagance in money and dress were further abuses. The Tory swells of the High Borlace Club, with their money and their insufferable arrogance, set a standard of expense which was ruinous to their imitators. Tick abounded; the tailor and the coffee-house fastened their burden of debt upon every undergraduate who fell into their hands.

How much of all this can have been true? Amhurst was a satirist, who wrote for effect; but it does not follow that he was an absolute liar. Much of what he describes is still true to-day. Oxford is still the scene of some heavy drinking; and with its execrable climate, it is likely to remain so. The Oxford tradesmen are still permitted to ensnare the young by way of high prices and boundless credit; indeed, the scandalous expense of lodgings is an extortion added on since Amhurst's day. In any age, a community of thousands of young men will force some relaxation of monastic standards.

Undoubtedly, the eighteenth-century dons often set a bad example. Their tenure was secure, sometimes irremovable. The exaction of an oath of allegiance which few honest churchmen could take meant that the plums of office went to the easy-going time-servers. Nepotism was common, sometimes even statutory; by the terms of Chichele's statutes, for instance, more than half the fellows of All Souls were " founders' kin," elected for no other reason. Celibacy was imposed upon the fellows; and many of them preferred to contrive a liaison with some wench below stairs rather than lose a comfortable sinecure. When the fellows of All Souls employed the university's own press for pornographic ends; when the Provost of Worcester could be seen " in the great window next the quadrangle," " seen by Mr. Dean himself and almost all the house," in company with a Madam Walcup, " toyeing with her most ridiculously and fanning himself with her fan for almost all the afternoon "—it was not to be hoped that the junior members of the university should observe much higher standards, or spurn the advances of the tradesmen's daughters.

Some heads of houses made very light of their duties. Hearne records that Mr. George Wigan, the Principal of New Inn Hall, has shut up the gate of it, and lives wholly in the country. Mr. Wightwicke was Master of Pembroke, doubtless as " founders' kin," since he bore the same name as the co-founder; he was " famed for a great Racer," and conducted the college services " with incredible Swiftness and confused Rapidity " as if he was running a race. A seventeenth-century canon of Christ Church, " a boon companion," preached upon one of the New Testament miracles to this effect : " every good fellow could turn wine into water ; but who or any mortal could turn water into wine. This I say makes the miracle the greater."

Though the modern examination system has proved a very mixed blessing, there was little merit in the methods by which degrees were awarded in the eighteenth century. The qualifications were in theory both doctrinal and scholastic, and the former consisted in reading the 39 Articles. " The Dean of the College invites the young man to breakfast—a couple of articles are read —then succeeds a wadding of cold meat—an interlayer of boiled eggs divides the third and fourth ; the doctrine of Predestination requires to be swallowed down with a cup of tea, and the Dean reads the newspaper, while the candidate reads the remainder." As for scholastic qualifications, their scrutiny was a pure formality. The proctors selected the examiners, and by paying a crown to the proctor's man, the candidate could get the examiner he wanted. Amhurst says that " it is the custom for the candidates to present the examiners with a piece of gold, or to give them a handsome entertainment, and make them drunk ; which they commonly do the night before examination, and sometimes keep them till morning, and so adjourn, cheek by jowl, from their drinking room to the school where they are to be examined." A few stock questions, with answers " handed down from age to age," were then set to the examinee ; his testimonium was signed ; and a few weeks later he found himself a Bachelor of Arts.

The drinking was undoubtedly terrific. Mr. Inett, a gentleman commoner of Magdalen Hall, drank himself to death at a drinking-party ; as for Lord Lovelace, the Principal of his hall " never knew him sober but twelve hours," which is not surprising, since he drank a quart of brandy every morning.

An excellent picture of the Oxford parson, entirely convincing because of its ingenuousness, is drawn by that observant traveller, Pastor Moritz, as late as 1782. Moritz was a Lutheran pastor, the son of a regimental oboist at Hameln ; his sophistication was small ; and he travelled through Georgian England with wide-open eyes, on foot. He had high hopes of Oxford, " that seat of the muses " ; but as a foot-traveller, he got short shrift from the taverns on the way, where he was refused admittance. Past Nuneham, late at night, he was overtaken by a jovial companion who announced himself as the curate of Dorchester ; and they proceeded into Oxford together. Moritz was tired out ; and it was midnight when they arrived in " the longest, the finest, and most beautiful street in Europe." The curate, Mr. Modd, was sustained by the hope of still finding company in an ale-house, and accordingly they looked in at the Mitre, where Moritz saw to his astonishment " a great number of clergymen, all with their gowns and bands on, sitting around a large table, each with his pot of beer before him." The conversation was " loud, general, and a little confused." One Mr. Clerk started " sundry objections to the Bible." First he maintained that the Bible said " that God was a *wine-bibber*, and a *drunkard*."

" On this Mr. Modd fell into a violent passion, and maintained that it was utterly impossible that any such passage should be found in the Bible. Another Divine, a Mr. Caern, referred us to his absent brother, who had already been forty years in the church, and must certainly know something of such a passage, if it were in the Bible, but he would venture to lay any wager his brother knew nothing of it.

" ' Waiter ! Fetch a Bible ! ' called out Mr. Clerk, and a great family Bible was immediately brought in, and opened on the table, among all the beer jugs. Mr. Clerk turned over a few leaves, and in the Book of Judges he read : ' Shall I leave my wine, which cheereth God and man ? '

" Mr. Modd and Mr. Caern, who had before been most violent, now sat as if struck dumb. A silence of some minutes prevailed, when all at once I said, ' Why, gentlemen, you must be sensible, that is but an allegorical expression ; how often, in the Bible, are Kings called Gods ? '

" ' Why, yes, to be sure,' said Mr. Modd and Mr. Caern, ' it is an allegorical expression ; nothing can be more clear ; it is a metaphor, and therefore it is absurd to understand it in a literal sense.' And now they, in their turn, triumphed over poor Clerk, and drank large draughts to my health. Mr. Clerk, however, had not yet exhausted his quiver ; and so he desired them to explain to him a passage in the prophecy of Isaiah, where it is said, in express terms, that *God is a barber*. Mr. Modd was so enraged at this, that he called Clerk an impudent fellow ; and Mr. Caern again still more earnestly referred us to his absent brother, who had been forty years in the church ; and who therefore, he doubted not, would also consider Mr. Clerk as an impudent fellow, if he maintained any such abominable notions. Mr. Clerk, all this while, sat perfectly composed ; but turning to a passage in Isaiah, he read these words : ' In the same day, the Lord shall shave with a razor the head, and the hair of the feet ; and it shall also consume the beard.' If Mr. Modd and Mr. Caern were before stunned and confounded, they were much more so now. I broke silence a second time and said : ' Why, gentlemen, this also is clearly metaphorical, and it is equally just, strong, and beautiful.' ' Aye, to be sure it is,' rejoined Mr. Modd and Mr. Caern, both in a breath ; at the same time, rapping the table with their knuckles. ' Aye to be sure it is ; anybody may see it is ; why, it is as clear as the day.' . . . Mr. Clerk made no further objections to the Bible. My health, however, was again encored and drank in strong ale. . . . At last when morning drew near, Mr. Modd suddenly exclaimed, ' Damn me, I must read prayers this morning at All Souls ! ' "

Mr. Modd was in fact the chaplain of Corpus, whose President and Fellows once had to admonish him for his drunkenness.

Moritz's photographic impression of the futility of the lesser clergy is really far more striking than the celebrated and sonorous denunciation of Edward Gibbon. Gibbon went up to Magdalen

61 " College Service " from a drawing by Thomas Rowlandson

62, 63   The Radcliffe Observatory, Ackermann's and Rowlandson's Views

in 1752, when he was not quite fifteen years old. He kept four terms before his conversion to the catholic faith made it impossible for him to return.

" To the university of Oxford *I* acknowledge no obligation ; and she will as cheerfully renounce me for a son, as I am willing to disclaim her for a mother. I spent fourteen months at Magdalen College ; they proved the fourteen months the most idle and unprofitable of my whole life : the reader will pronounce between the school and the scholar ; but I cannot affect to believe that Nature had disqualified me for all literary pursuits. . . . The fellows of my time were decent easy men, who supinely enjoyed the gifts of the founder ; their days were filled by a series of uniform employments ; the chapel and the hall, the coffee-house and the common room, till they retired, weary and well satisfied, to a long slumber. From the toil of reading, or thinking, or writing, they had absolved their conscience ; and the first shoots of learning and ingenuity withered on the ground, without yielding any fruits to the owners or the public. As a gentleman commoner, I was admitted to the society of the fellows, and fondly expected that some questions of literature would be the amusing and instructive topics of their discourse. Their conversation stagnated in a round of college business, Tory politics, personal anecdotes, and private scandal : their dull and deep potations excused the brisk intemperance of youth ; and their constitutional toasts were not expressive of the most lively loyalty for the House of Hanover."

All these fine sentences betray his self-centred and censorious mind. Gibbon was a home-bred prodigy before he went up to Oxford, and he hoped too much. Let us counterbalance his experience with that of another man of still more active mind. Charles James Fox came from Eton to Hertford in 1764. The head of his college was Dr. Newcome, " a good, wise, and learned divine." Fox was rich and profligate ; he had a multitude of Eton friends, with whom he shared a mania for cards : yet he read so intensively at Oxford that Dr. Newcome had to implore him to desist. At Oxford, he acquired a considerable culture and a boundless intellectual appetite. Gibbon was always a weakling ; but Fox showed himself as tough in the physical as in the intellectual sphere. At the end of term he came home on foot from Oxford to Kensington.

Fox's friend and contemporary, Lord Malmesbury, found his two years at Merton " most unprofitably spent." " A gentleman commoner was under no restraint, and never called upon to attend either lectures, chapel, or hall. My tutor, an excellent and worthy man, gave himself no concern about his pupils." Such criticism assumes that the university should base itself like a public school upon a system of compulsion ; whereas it has always been the merit of Oxford that it leaves the learner to seek out knowledge for himself.

A class of men who came to Oxford determined to make the

best use of their time were the " servitors," known to their masters as " barbers." These were poor scholars from country grammar schools and the like, who worked their way through the university on a capital of a few pounds. Their presence was tolerated on the terms that they should fetch and carry meals, clean shoes, and shave their more fortunate brethren. Their learning was also employed in writing essays and declamations on behalf of others. " Impositions " were still in use as a penalty at Oxford, as they are to-day in more conservative schools; but as a matter of course the independent undergraduate would depute his servitor to " barbarise " his imposition for a few shillings.

George Whitefield, whose fame was to resound on both sides of the Atlantic, was a servitor at Pembroke; in this capacity he found his previous experience in the Bell Inn at Gloucester of great use to him. The father of the three Wesleys was a servitor at Exeter. These men did not make sacrifices and face great hardships for the sake of a worthless degree at a decadent university. If they were so earnest to pick up the crumbs, there must have been some sustenance on the table. Old Wesley showed his own sense of obligation by sending all his three sons, John, Samuel, and Charles, to be educated at Christ Church.

John Wesley remained for some years as a fellow of Lincoln, and was invited to preach before the university even after the inception of methodism. But Oxford would repel with horror any suggestion that it was the cradle of Wesleyanism.

The most celebrated undergraduate of the eighteenth century was Samuel Johnson. He came up from his humble home at Lichfield to Pembroke in 1728. He was almost penniless, and extremely proud. " Ah, Sir, I was mad and violent. It was bitterness which they mistook for frolick. I was miserably poor, and I thought to fight my way by my literature and my wit; so I disregarded all power and all authority."

He had a friend, one Taylor, across the road in lordly Christ Church. " Mr. Bateman's lectures were so excellent that Johnson used to come and get them at second hand from Taylor, till his poverty being so extreme that his shoes were worn out, and his feet appeared through them, he saw that this humiliating circumstance was perceived by the Christ Church men, and he came no more. He was too proud to accept of money, and somebody having set a pair of new shoes at his door, he threw them away with indignation."

Of his tutor, Johnson said that " he was a very worthy man, but a heavy man, and I did not profit much by his instructions. Indeed, I did not attend him much." Sent for to explain why he had absented himself from four successive tutorials, Johnson explained with much nonchalance that he had been sliding in Christ Church meadows.

" *Boswell.* That, Sir, was great fortitude of mind.
Johnson. No, Sir ; stark insensibility."

Johnson's time at Oxford was not only unhappy, but short. He kept barely four terms : yet the pages of Boswell are full of his praises both for his university and his college. He loved to revisit the place. Showing the sights of Pembroke to Hannah More, he would explain how many poets the college had produced —" we are a nest of singing-birds." Dr. Routh, who as President of Magdalen lived until 1854, once saw Johnson going up the steps of University; while University, by his own account, once witnessed him drink three bottles of port without being the worse for it.

Assuredly it was no mere sentimentality that bound Johnson so closely to Oxford. It may have been that if some chance had sent him to Cambridge, Johnson might have developed into a canting Whig. As it was, the Toryism which lay so deep in his nature made him love Oxford as the great home of Toryism. But it was a form of political faith which underwent much evolution even in Johnson's lifetime. As a student, he was of Jacobite sympathies, fitting in one who had been touched for the King's evil by the last of the Stuarts. In his day probably a majority of members of the university remained Jacobites. The tradition died hard. As late as 1746, the opening of the Radcliffe Library was the occasion of a furious Jacobite harangue by the Principal of St. Mary Hall. It was George III who skilfully disarmed his enemies at last by reviving a Tory party. Neither of his predecessors had visited Oxford ; and indeed there would have been riots if they had. But George III was able to come down in 1786, with Fanny Burney tittering in his retinue, and the occasion passed off with great success.

Johnson had by then long since made his peace with the House of Hanover. But the Tory prejudice still held fast to its ancient victim, the dissenter. At Oxford, the tests were maintained in all their severity, not to be abolished for another century. Johnson heartily approved of them. In 1768, a group of six dissenters was expelled from St. Edmund Hall on this account. Boswell thought this measure harsh, and lamely pleaded that he had heard they were " good beings." " *Johnson.* I believe they might be good beings, but they were not fit to be in the University of Oxford. A cow is a very good animal in a field, but we turn her out of a garden."

He carried this prejudice into the smallest concerns of life: " One day when Dr. Johnson and Sir Robert Chambers were together in the garden of New Inn Hall, Sir Robert occupied himself in collecting snails and throwing them over the wall into the adjoining premises. The Doctor thereupon reprimanded him, and

pronounced his behaviour unmannerly and unneighbourly.
'Sir!' said Sir Robert, 'my neighbour is a Dissenter.' 'Oh!'
exclaimed the Doctor, 'if so, my dear Chambers, toss away, toss
away as hard as you can!'"

64 (*opposite*): The Wrought-Iron
Gates of New College Garden

Classical Oxford
as it is

T HE CHARACTERISTIC OF ALL THIS LONG PERIOD IS THE CON-
viction of all those who lived in it that by no apparent means
could their world, their lives, or their culture be improved.
They never doubted that their age was the best of all possible
ages ; nor, in a smaller sphere, that the University of Oxford had
attained the ultimate perfection possible in a place of learning. It
was large, rich, and famous ; one asked no more. And that
is the reason why, in two centuries, but one new college was
established.

Though a complacent, it was an unheroic age. There was no
lack of glory in the wars of Marlborough, nor of courage in the
exploits of Clive. Architecture was lavish, proud, monumental.
The university might stand in need of no improvement ; but it
was handsomely adorned by grateful generations. To the em-
bellishment of Oxford were devoted the talents of several amateur
architects of high merit. Oxford produced and fostered the
greatest English architect of all.

Wren had his first big chance in Oxford. At the age of thirty
he enjoyed a European reputation as a mathematician. As
Savilian Professor of Astronomy, he was contriving lenses, globes,
and pendula—the more mature successors of his sundials and way-
wisers. In the course of his work he had delivered a series of
lectures on the Geometrical Flat Floor. He was now commissioned
to erect a " flat floor " of uncommon size.

Gilbert Sheldon, Archbishop of Canterbury, was distressed and
shocked by the irreverence of the annual Encænia at Oxford.
The licence accorded to Terræ Filius and the other buffoons was
broad, and based on old tradition. It was all very well, but this
coarse mummery took place at yearly intervals within the consecrated walls of St. Mary's, as the university church. Hopeless
of purifying the proceedings, Sheldon decided to transfer them to
a secular setting, and for this purpose to erect a theatre. It was
here that Christopher Wren's researches proved useful. The

11 69

65 (*opposite*) : Tom Tower, Christ Church

amphitheatres of the ancients had no ceilings, set as they were beneath blue Mediterranean skies. How was it possible, given the standard size of timber, to cover in a theatre of the classic shape and size ? It had never been done. The broadest span in Oxford was in Christ Church Hall, where great Irish oak-beams bridged a space of forty feet. The hall was essentially a quadrilateral : what Sheldon aimed at was a semicircle. He decided to risk his scheme on the professor's Geometrical Flat Floor.

The Sheldonian Theatre is not really a beautiful building. A grotesque and pedantic row of mouldering heads of Roman worthies strikes an unfortunate note in the view of the curved front to the north, from which side, also, the composition by its very nature can nowhere be satisfactorily taken in. The south front is more successful. Here is the ceremonial entrance, aligned to the position of the Divinity School. It was to provide access across to this entrance that Wren boldly provided the Divinity School with a north door.

The interior of the Sheldonian is delightful. With its curious boxes, pulpits, and galleries, all of the most Wrennish carpentry, it is as odd a theatre as any in the world. It is of course adapted particularly for the curious ceremonies of the university—annual occasions when degrees are given, when Latin compliments are bandied, when prize poems are read, and when the distant lodging-houses of North Oxford send forth their camphor-scented array of strange anchorites and learned nobodies.

The ceiling of the theatre is seventy feet by eighty : by an extremely happy pretence this is adorned with foreshortened painting which purports to be strung upon ropes, as though it were an awning slung across the open amphitheatre. Wren's portrait is to be seen above one of the boxes. The organ and its case are the work of Sir T. G. Jackson.

A staircase in the corner of the building gives access to the cupola on the roof ; but it is not so good a view-point, except in wet weather, as the roof of the Radcliffe Camera. The great loft below the cupola is certainly worth seeing ; for here are the beams and trusses which enabled Wren to effect his architectural innovation. To throw off the shackles of a narrow roof-span, limited by the size of available timber, was a departure comparable to the introduction of ferro-concrete. A model of the building was exhibited in London, for the admiration of the Royal Society.

Among these huge timbers the University Press established its workshop when the Theatre was first built. For many years the " Theatre " was the imprint sign of Oxford books. Here the fellows of All Souls pored furtively over their secret proofs of Aretin's *Postures*.

John Evelyn came to Oxford in October 1664, and was handsomely entertained for two days. He found Wren in the former observatory at the top of the Old Schools Tower " with an inverted tube, or telescope, observing the discus of the sun for the passing of Mercury that day before it." They strolled across to the Bodleian, where the librarian showed Evelyn his name among the benefactors. From there Wren took him to see the foundations of " the new Theatre, now building at an exceeding and royal expense by the Lord Archbishop of Canterbury . . . the whole designed by that incomparable genius, my worthy friend Dr. Christopher Wren, who showed me the model, not disdaining my advice in some particulars." That day he also looked in to see the new painting in All Souls chapel, where the old reredos had been, and found it " too full of nakeds for a chapel." Five years later, Evelyn was present when the Theatre was opened with an Encænia, which " drew a world of strangers." The poor man was terribly shocked when " Terræ Filius entertained the auditory with a tedious, abusive, sarcastical rhapsody, most unbecoming the gravity of the University. . . . It was rather licentious lying and railing than genuine and noble wit. In my life, I was never witness of so shameful entertainment." Sheldon's £25,000 was in his view well spent in freeing St. Mary's sacred walls from such ribaldry as this. Though the office of buffoon has died away, the Encænia was till quite lately an uproarious event, attended by multitudes of undergraduates. Nowadays it is decorous and dull. Between whiles, the Theatre is used for some of the many excellent musical performances with which Oxford is surpassingly provided and enriched. Schnabel and Kreisler play on the same boards as Handel and his lousy crew of foreign fiddlers.

Wren's next employment was just across the street, at Trinity. This college, Carolean in its present aspect, still occupied the ancient buildings of Durham College, the former Benedictine settlement, taken over as they were by Sir Thomas Pope when he founded the new college in 1555. There had been added since then a dingy hall, and a curious gabled row of buildings called Kettell Hall, which still flanks the college front, with its own separate porch on Broad Street. The name of this block derives from Dr. Kettell, the President of Trinity whose end was hastened by the outrageous licence of the Court ladies during the Civil Wars. Kettell has been so well described by John Aubrey, his own pupil, that a digression is not to be avoided.

" The Doctor's fashion was to go up and down the college, and peep in at the keyholes to see whether the boys did follow their books or no.

" He observed that the houses that had the smallest beer had the most drunkards, for it forced them to go into the town to comfort their stomachs, wherefore Dr. Kettel always had in his college excellent beer, not better to be had in Oxon, so that we could not go to any other place but for the worse, and we had the fewest drunkards of any house in Oxford.

"He preached every Sunday at his parsonage at Garsington, about five miles off. He rode on his bay gelding, with his boy Ralph before him, with a leg of mutton (commonly) and some college bread.

"A neighbour of mine, Mr. St. Low, told me he heard him preach once in St. Mary's Church at Oxon. I know not whether this was the only time or no that he used this following way of conclusion : But now I see it is time for me to shut up my book, for I see the doctors' men coming wiping of their beards from the alehouse. (He could from the pulpit plainly see them, and 'twas their custom in sermon to go there, and about the end of sermon to return to wait on their masters.)

"Our Grove was the Daphne for the ladies and their gallants to walk in, and many times my lady Isabella Thynne would make her entry with a theorbo or lute played before her. . . . She was the most beautiful, most humble, charitable, etc., but she could not subdue one thing. I remember one time this lady and fine Mrs. Fenshawe (her great and intimate friend, who lay at our college) would have a frolic to make a visit to the President. The old Dr. quickly perceived that they came to abuse him : he addresses his discourse to Mrs. Fenshawe, saying, Madam, your husband and father I bred up here, and I knew your grandfather. I know you to be a gentlewoman, I will not say you are a whore ; but get you gone for a very woman. The dissoluteness of the times, as I have said, grieving the good old Doctor, his days were shortened, and died and was buried at Garsington."

Kettell was succeeded after the Restoration by a kinsman, Dr. Ralph Bathurst, one of whose first acts as President was to summon his friend and fellow-scientist Wren to advise him on the enlargement of the college. Before his death, forty years later, Bathurst had practically rebuilt the whole of it.

The front quadrangle of Trinity is a kind of orchard. The focal point is a pair of entrance gates, perpetually closed, which were presented by the father of the famous Lord North. To the left are the repulsive buildings of Balliol ; in front, a fine classic chapel ; while the remainder is predominantly, and by this time I hope obviously, the work of Sir T. G. Jackson, except for the tumbledown cottages along Broad Street.

If you cross the quad and pass under the clock tower of the chapel, you come into the oldest part of Trinity. This is a bare quadrangle containing a very old library and a Jacobean hall. Through and beyond this to the north are the extensions in which Wren assisted. His advice had been to build a " lame quadrangle," that is to say, a quadrangle with one side open to let in the light and air. In this respect Wren set a fashion which was immediately copied by William Bird in his additions to New College, and by Hawksmoor at Queen's and All Souls. But the only portion which Wren actually built was the north wing ; and that has been altered

66 The Screen of Busts of the Roman Emperors round the Sheldonian
(The building behind this pair is the Old Ashmolean)

67 The Interior of the Sheldonian

out of all recognition. What he built, in about 1665, was an independent block, with mullioned windows, a pediment, dormers, and a Mansard roof—the last being a new-fangled French importation of his own. Some fifteen years later the west side was added, and sixty years later the south side ; so that Wren's work has been assimilated into the scheme, while losing all its individual features.

The garden upon which this quadrangle opens is very fine. At the far end is a gate corresponding to that on Broad Street : there is a legend that it is never to be opened except to admit a Stuart sovereign. Both pairs of gates were made by Thomas Robinson, the craftsman of the New College grille. The iron spikes which surmount them, and the array of broken bottles set in cement along the adjoining walls, convey a vivid idea of the fortifications required by every college. In spite of these obstacles, Trinity is reputed the easiest college to enter after twelve. There is an attractive lime-walk on the south side of the garden. The old pictures showed a maze or labyrinth on this side. No doubt this part of the garden was the " Grove " where Lady Isabella Thynne would make her entry with a theorbo or lute played before her. A more serious note is now struck by the bust of Cardinal Newman.

To return, through both quadrangles, to the chapel, this was the last of Dr. Bathurst's embellishments. The old chapel was destroyed in 1691, by which time Wren's architectural practice had passed all bounds. The work was entrusted to none other than the Dean of Christ Church, Dr. Henry Aldrich. It is one of the most successful things in Oxford.

It is pleasing to imagine what would transpire to-day if the head of one college were asked to design the chapel of another. Aldrich was an amiable divine, renowned as a smoker of tobacco, and as a composer of anthems and musical catches, of which " The Bonnie Christ Church Bells " is the best known. He bequeathed a large musical library to the House. He was his own architect for the Peckwater Quadrangle ; later still, he built All Saints' Church. But Trinity chapel appears to have been his first, as it is his best work.

The front of the chapel is most exquisitely proportioned. The requirements of size called for no more than four bays—always a number to be avoided by any architect of skill. Aldrich avoided it with perfect dexterity. There should be a kind of *porte-cochère* to prolong the mass of the building. Its character as an entrance should be accentuated by an extra storey ; and lest it should seem to masquerade uncomfortably as an ante-chapel, belfry, or anything of that sort, its secular character is further emphasised by rectangular sash windows. For symmetry, an arch is introduced ; for distinction, the head of this arch is filled in. Finally, and with

12   73

what art, the line of the principal roof is renewed and prolonged beyond the little tower, for exactly the right distance. How surely is the whole structure buttressed, anchored, and balanced, by the extrusion of those five feet or so of stonework.

Wren, as a very old friend of Dr. Bathurst, was asked to look over Aldrich's design. It seems that he slightly altered the balustrade, and suggested the gay vases in place of some more formal type of pinnacle. For the rest, it was a plan which he might have been proud to own himself.

If the exterior of this building charms, its interior dazzles ; for it contains a fantastic profusion of the finest work of Grinling Gibbons. At the east end, his limewood carvings surround fine panels of veneer beneath a broken curved pediment. The wainscots of the side walls are of oak. They terminate in a pair of glazed cupboards, ingeniously contrived so that the tomb of the founder, a revered but incongruous object, might remain at hand and open to inspection without obtruding its primitive appearance in such a setting. The screen at the west end is also ornamented by Grinling Gibbons ; and its two seats of honour, with their little canopies, are singularly neat and pleasing. The candles, the plaster roof, and the marble floor complete an effect which by some miracle has survived the attentions of the nineteenth century, unspoiled except by some detestable stained glass.

Having transformed and embellished his college, Ralph Bathurst died in the fortieth year of his Presidency. When he had finished with building, there was one other pleasure left to him, and this was to observe the desolate state of Balliol College next door. " Dr. Bathurst was perhaps secretly pleased to see a neighbouring and once a rival society reduced to this condition, while his own flourished beyond all others. Accordingly, one afternoon he was found in his garden, which then ran almost contiguous to the east side of Balliol-college, throwing stones at the windows with much satisfaction, as if happy to contribute his share in completing the appearance of its ruin."

Tom Tower, Wren's Oxford masterpiece, was designed at the height of his fame, fifteen years after the Great Fire of London. It used to be confidently stated that he was the architect of the Old Ashmolean, that charming little museum which stands alongside his Sheldonian, to which it is rather more than ten years junior. Nowadays this attribution is challenged. The Old Ashmolean is intended as an unpretentious building, and the Broad Street front is modest enough ; but on the eastern entrance the architect, whoever he may be, lets himself go with a pyramidal flight of steps and a massive pediment, curved in more directions than one, all centring round a doorway of quite ordinary size. It is a very successful piece of architectural exaggeration, and the detail is admirably carried out. It is interesting to compare this

69   Christ Church and Tom Tower, from a drawing by J. M. W. Turner
(*ca.* 1794)

70   The Doorway of the
Old Ashmolean

71   The Clarendon and Sheldonian Buildings

72   The Clarendon Building, with a glimpse of the new Bodleian

work with the Sheldonian : it bears no intrinsic unlikeness to Wren's work, and would suggest that his skill and confidence had grown in the intervening period.

The Old Ashmolean was built to house a collection of curiosities formed in the seventeenth century by two famous gardeners and botanists, both employed by Charles I, namely, the two John Tradescants, father and son. They formed a " physic garden " at Lambeth ; but their natural history collection descended to Elias Ashmole, an eccentric and astrologer, who presented his own and the Tradescant collections to the university. They have formed the nucleus of a much larger collection, which has long since moved its quarters. The main floor of the Old Ashmolean now houses the offices of the Oxford English Dictionary. The upper storey, to which access is obtained by a side entrance, contains an interesting collection of scientific instruments ; but from an architectural standpoint the interior is of no interest.

The Sheldonian's other neighbour carries the story on for yet another thirty years. The Clarendon Building was finished just fifty years after the Sheldonian was begun. It was built to house the university printing press, for which the Theatre had become an insufficient home. Hyde, Earl of Clarendon and Chancellor of Oxford, had written a best-seller in his *History of the Rebellion*, as all haunters of old bookshops may observe. His son, Lord Cornbury, the friend of John Evelyn and High Steward of Oxford, gave the copyright of this valuable work to the university. This sudden bounty was promptly used to build the " Clarendon." The design appears to have originated in a sketch by Sir John Vanbrugh carried out by Nicholas Hawksmoor. The former was engaged on Blenheim Palace at the time, and doubtless had frequent occasion to visit Oxford. The latter was a distinguished pupil in the office of Sir Christopher Wren, who was then almost retired, having seen the completion of St. Paul's.

The University Press, whose continuous history dates from 1583, only remained in the Clarendon building for just a century before it had to transfer, like the Ashmolean, to larger premises. It is worth recording that the beautiful types which this press still uses were collected by Dr. Fell, who was fond of having books printed for his private circulation. The Clarendon building now contains the principal university offices, and most notably those of the proctors. On any morning in term, undergraduates are to be seen in cap and gown attending to learn the penalty of their transgression. They are summoned by tickets sent to their colleges. Some ten years ago, Mr. Duncan Sandys contrived to have such tickets distributed to almost the whole university ; and the following morning the Clarendon was besieged by an indignant mob of several hundreds. But such enterprise is rare.

We have seen Hawksmoor's pseudo-Gothic quadrangle at All

Souls, and regretted the miscarriage of his scheme to rebuild Brasenose. But he had his great chance instead at Queen's, where he rebuilt the entire college to his own design.

Queen's was the sixth of Oxford colleges, being founded in the year 1340. It had become very rich, and its original quarters were three and a half centuries old; so the fellows decided that the requirements of a spacious age, in which the humblest student expected two large rooms, justified an entirely fresh start. Their first step was to build a library, and this was done in the 1690's. It is a little difficult to attribute this design exactly, since Hawksmoor was then actually in Wren's office. Like so much else that people have put down to Wren, it is most likely that the plans were sometimes glanced at by the great Surveyor-General, and that he made hints and criticisms upon them. Certain it is that all the remainder of the present college was designed by Hawksmoor himself after 1700, and finished about 1733.

The great front quadrangle of Queen's is three-sided, like those added to New College and Trinity; while the fourth side is linked up by a piazza, as in Hawksmoor's other effort at All Souls. The graceful dome over the entrance, in which columns are frankly employed as buttresses, shelters a statue of George II's brilliant Queen, Caroline of Anspach, who gave her blessing to the rebuilding. In this she carried forward a traditional association between the college and the queens of England which began with Queen Philippa and has not ceased with Queen Mary. The terminal pediments on either side are adorned with symbolical statues, as were those of the Clarendon building.

Within the quadrangle a massive arcade is carried round three sides, of which two are plain and solid blocks of "staircases." Facing the entrance are chapel and hall, aligned in one block, but in reversal of the usual order. The hall is to the left, a noble room of great height, marred by the alterations of Mr. Kempe. The chapel opens from the central passage opposite the gate, and protrudes an apsidal eastern end into Queen's Lane. In this severely classical composition, an incongruity is created by some old glass of the van Ling brothers, saved from the former chapel and but ill adapted to its present place. The ceiling of the apse is painted by Thornhill; the screen, with its particular ornate seat for the Provost, is carved by Grinling Gibbons; while the silver upon the altar is the handiwork of the greatest of all silversmiths, Paul Lamerie.

The second quadrangle at Queen's is a considerably plainer affair than the first, apart from its noble library. Those who know Wren's great library at Trinity College, Cambridge, will quickly understand why this work is so confidently attributed to the same hand; but it might equally well have been the triumph of a brilliant pupil. The Trinity library maintains its original

76

75 (*overleaf*): The Oxford Skyline from the Sheldonian Cupola

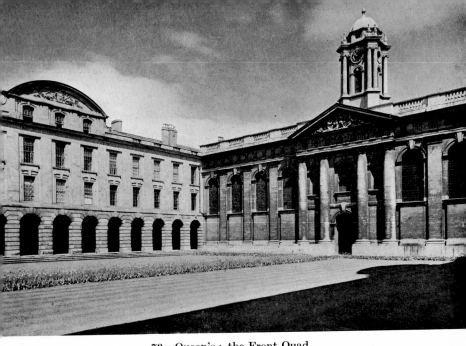

73   Queen's : the Front Quad

74   Queen's : the High Street Front

76   Queen's : the Library

77   Queen's : a Carved
      Panel from one of
      the Racks

feature of an open colonnade below, to protect the room from mildew and to provide a promenade for gossiping dons below. This golden intention, so often formed but as often departed from, has here again given way to the ceaseless expansion of the library. The ground floor is merely an untidy book-store. The room above it is one of the noblest libraries in England. In its layout the architect has reverted to the mediæval system of ranging the cases at right angles to the walls, so that between each pair is a secluded bay for study. A fine plaster ceiling and a quantity of Grinling Gibbons carvings scattered about the bookcase-ends complete the effect of lavish and cultivated luxury. Though nothing can quite compare with the three old parts of the Bodleian, though the Christ Church library (some twenty years later) is more beautiful, Queen's library is the glory of the college, and since its recent restoration one of the best sights of Oxford.

Queen's maintains the connection with the counties of Westmorland and Cumberland which it derived from Robert Eglesfield, the founder. Many of the undergraduates are North Country; and in earlier days they found it necessary to winter in Oxford. For the Long Vacation, which of course was timed to coincide with the necessity of harvesting, they would revisit their distant homes ; but the state of the roads, and the distances, made this impossible at Christmas. To this day, though almost everybody is at St. Moritz or Madeira, there are Christmas celebrations at Queen's, with a boar's head and a special carol ; while on New Year's Day the bursar mysteriously presents a needle and thread to each of the other fellows. Queen's is the last of colleges to brew its own beer.

Contemporary with the great new works at Queen's, two other handsome additions to the High Street were made, and both by unprofessional architects. Almost next door, Dr. George Clarke built himself the Warden's house attached to the front of All Souls. At All Saints' Church, a couple of hundred yards along on the same side, Dean Aldrich was presented with a singular opportunity. In 1699 the tower collapsed and fell on to the church. It was rebuilt from his design in 1708. The site was at the foot of the Turl, and the new church was placed so that it almost touches the Mitre Hotel across the road. It may very well have been that Aldrich had some scheme to widen the Turl into a triumphal way between this church and his chapel at Trinity, whose unused gateway is aligned to such a layout. All Saints' could have stood astride of such a street as does St. Mary's in Radcliffe Square. But it was not to be : the Turl remains its dingy self.

All Saints' is not in the same class as Trinity chapel. The tower and spire are a laborious imitation of the inimitable forms that Wren contrived with so many variations for his City churches. The interior is like a hat-box seen from the moth's point of view, being almost as wide as it is long. It has been twice Victorianised ; and the windows are cluttered up with horrible stained glass. There is a fine pulpit, and a delightful monument to a centenarian alderman. All Saints' is the official church of the city, just as St. Mary's is of the university. On the first Sunday in each month the Mayor and Corporation come here in procession. The parish was amalgamated with St. Martin's when the old church at Carfax had to be pulled down. Amongst other relics, the font came from St. Martin's : this is the font in which Sir William Davenant was baptised with Shakespeare standing godfather ; though whether he attended in person, nobody knows.[1]

Aldrich died in 1710, but the remarkable group of talented amateurs did not die with him. Holdsworth made his bold plan for Magdalen, of which the New Buildings were erected in 1733. Dr. Clarke conceived his masterly scheme at All Souls, whereby the hall was to balance the chapel, and the library was to balance them both ; he built the mighty library at the House ; and at Worcester College he got the chance to build a whole foundation anew.

Worcester is a long way from the heart of Oxford, but as French guides say, *vaut le détour*. The Benedictines, arriving on the scene as early as 1283, thought it wise to establish this colony away from the giddy distractions of the mediæval town, and set it on the fringe of Beaumont Palace. Confiscated by Henry VIII, their property was occupied for a while by Bishop King, and later sold to Sir Thomas White, the founder of St. John's, who established it as St. John Baptist Hall, a satellite foundation to his college. It did not prosper, though it produced one famous son in Richard Lovelace. So unsuccessful was the hall that it was threatened with demolition through inability to pay the chimney-tax. Schemes were promoted—one being to endow it as a house for members of the Orthodox Church ; but the old buildings continued to moulder and decay. At last, in 1714, Sir Thomas Cookes, a baronet of Worcestershire, bequeathed £10,000 to found

---

[1] Davenant's father kept the Crown Inn at Carfax, where Shakespeare used to stop on his way to Stratford. Upon these premises, now number 3 the Cornmarket, some old wall-paintings were lately discovered in a front room which Shakespeare may have occupied. The room is now open to the public. Shakespeare was " exceedingly respected " on his annual visits, so much so that some thought him to be the father of the younger Davenant.

In the year 1675 the Crown Inn saw a remarkable defeat of the Dutch admiral, Van Tromp, who had so humiliated the British Navy. Tromp spent his time in Oxford " either in the brandy shop or tavern " in company with a butler and a plumber : but the dons defeated him. " Dr. Speed stayed in town on purpose to drink with him, which is the only thing he is good for . . . who mustering about five or six as able men as himself at wine and brandy got the Dutchman to the Crown Tavern, and there so plied him that at 12 at night they were fain to carry him to his lodgings."

78   Queen's : the Library from the Garden

79   All Souls : the Warden's House

80   Worcester : the Garden Front

81   The Mitre Inn

a college for the men of that county; and with this fund the university took over what remained.

Dr. Clarke not only gave his services as architect, but also helped considerably towards the funds. His plan was original. For once the college entrance is not on the street, but is approached between two balancing wings, consisting of chapel and hall. These are connected by an arcade, above which is the long narrow library. It is an ingenious plan, similar to that of the King's Inns at Dublin. Unfortunately, the chapel has been ruined by an incredibly bad restoration; and its glass is now so murkily stained that it is almost impossible to judge what its appearance can have been. The library contains Clarke's admirable collection of architectural drawings.

Clarke died before his plans were carried out, and the completion of them was entrusted to Henry Keene, a professional architect. To him is due the great classical block of rooms adjoining the central group, and pompously overlooking the sunk quadrangle. With the existing levels, this layout is all the better for its unfinished state. It was undoubtedly intended to erect a south wing to balance the north; but money ran out, and the ramshackle little row of houses on the left was spared. These are the original " mansions " of Gloucester College, and the shields upon their doorways show how each represented an offshoot of some different abbey. Abingdon, Westminster, St. Albans, and so forth—each had its own entrance under its own coat-of-arms. Has it struck you as strange that undergraduates' rooms never open off a corridor, but always off a staircase of their own ? Here is the reason. The Benedictines built this way in the thirteenth century; and what they started still appears to be the best arrangement in the interests of peace and quiet. In the womens' colleges, they slouch about the long corridors and shuffle in and out of each other's rooms with gossip and cups of cocoa; but a man can retreat behind his impenetrable oak, and ward away all comers. If he wants to visit a friend, he must cross the quad to do it; but he will be able to make his visit in peace, immune from communal hilarity.

By an obscure hole in the south wall, you can get to the back of the " mansions," from which side their appearance is still more charmingly untidy. But they are not merely quaint; they contain some remarkable varieties of mediæval stonework. Following the garden walk, you arrive at a considerable artificial lake, contrived out of a swamp about a hundred years ago, which is Worcester's principal distinction. It is mournfully landscaped, and the only lake in Oxford; its proximity to two grubby railways and a canal adds a touch of sadness, as to some vista in Regent's Park.

In Walton Street, adjoining Worcester chapel, can be seen the old entrance to Gloucester College. A Victorian plan to rebuild the whole street front, by Mr. Blore of all men, was averted by want of money.

Even what there is of Worcester took over sixty years a-building, and ran short for money at that. No other college was founded for well over a century. The age was lacking in Waynfletes or Wolseys. There was little piety and less celibacy about. But the century produced one jolly bachelor, a highly representative figure, who left a considerable mark on Oxford. Dr. John Radcliffe graduated at University College, and practised medicine in Oxford. His knowledge of the subject was not specially great; but his wit was so exquisitely amusing that people feigned illness in order to get him in for a chat. Armed with such valuable powers, he transferred to London, and was soon earning twenty guineas a day. His fees were enormous for the times. He was perpetually being retained by members of the royal family, and as frequently sacked for his familiarities. He infuriated Queen Anne by saying that her malady was nothing but the vapours; and he got into trouble for not attending when summoned to her deathbed. He only survived her by three months.

We meet Dr. Radcliffe in all the diaries of the time. He was always open-handed with his money. Though he had resigned a fellowship at Lincoln rather than take orders himself, he freely helped the poor clergy. When Obadiah Walker was Master of Univ., Radcliffe gave him an east window for his chapel; and when he had to resign, Radcliffe pensioned him off. He made large gifts to St. Bartholomew's Hospital in London; but Oxford was his first loyalty, and got the bulk of his bequests.

To University College, Radcliffe left the money for the extensions to the college, and for certain fellowships and a library. His collection of medical works he left to the university with a sum of money to house and endow a library. Out of the surplus of their wealth, the Radcliffe Trustees later built an infirmary and an observatory, both of which are situated in the Woodstock Road. The infirmary is a plain handsome house designed by the same Henry Keene who finished off Clarke's plans at Worcester. It has been frequently extended with the growth of Oxford's population, and in the last few years has received such gigantic sums of money from Lord Nuffield that it is supposed to contain almost as many doctors as patients. This great accretion of wealth has meant still more buildings, with the unfortunate result that the observatory next door has been swallowed up. Its astronomical activities have been shifted to South Africa. A maternity wing obstructs its outlook; a Nuffield Professor of Therapeutics occupies the Astronomers' House. Unknown rites take place in the tall rooms where the telescopes used to be. But it is still worth seeing for its outside alone. Built between 1772 and 1795, it is almost the only late eighteenth-century work in Oxford ; and it is the first Greek revival work in Oxford. It is supposed to be reminiscent of a Temple of the Winds in Athens ; and there are some carvings of winds on the octagonal tower. But the charm of the building is in its solid squat base, relieved with niches and without a cornice, and in the *piano nobile* effect of the next storey, and in the immense windows of the room above, rendering the whole tower transparent. Nowadays observatories look like toadstools ; there is something pleasingly naïf about building a tower to be closer to the stars, with a lot of big windows to see them through.

The architect for the Astronomers' House and the Observatory was Henry Keene ; but the tower of the latter was completed by James Wyatt in his best Grecian manner. Anyone who compares it with Wyatt's other works in Oxford, namely, the library at Oriel and Canterbury Gate at the House, will find it difficult to believe that Wyatt did not design the whole building.

Further explorations north of the Observatory will prove disappointing to an architectural observer ; but on the return journey, by St. Giles's, there is a sight worth seeing in number 16, on the east side of the street. This house is the Judges' Lodgings ; that is to say, the tenant makes way for a High Court Judge at every Oxford assize. It is an excellent Queen Anne specimen, bearing the date 1702 on its lead fittings. The architect is unknown ; but it seems that Sarah Duchess of Marlborough rented the house at one period.[1]

Dr. Radcliffe's " Physic " Library was nobly accommodated in the most conspicuous building in Oxford, the great domed " Camera " in Radcliffe Square. The Doctor left £40,000 for the purpose, and it is easy to suppose that it was swallowed up in the erection of this vast rotunda. James Gibbs was the architect ; he is better known for his work at Cambridge and some London churches. His work began in 1739, and ended eight years later. It is more ponderous than beautiful in effect.

The mighty rustic base with its iron grilles was intended as an open space, in accordance with precedent ; but as always, it has been filled in. Not only that, but the whole square has been dug up and great underground bookstores have been constructed, from which it takes about an hour to fetch a book. The Physics Library, of which Radcliffe was so proud, has been ousted altogether, and sent away to a science museum. The Camera has become the central reading-room of the Bodleian. Hence these rows of bicycles ; hence the stream of young women trooping like bees in and out of a hive. By following them up fine curved stairs you

[1] St. Giles's is the scene of one of the greatest of England's country fairs, on September 5th and 6th in each year.

come to the great circular room, with its depressing groups of desks and still more depressing miles of catalogues. From this level a corkscrew stair leads up to the open leads of the roof. The view from this high balustrade is one of the most striking things in Oxford. There is also a whimsical view into the Camera itself through the big windows of the drum.

82 (*opposite*) : All Souls : Hawksmoor's Pinnacles from the Radcliffe Camera

83   All Souls : the Codrington Library

84   All Souls : Hawksmoor's Towers

85   Magdalen : the New Building

86   All Souls : the Inner Quad

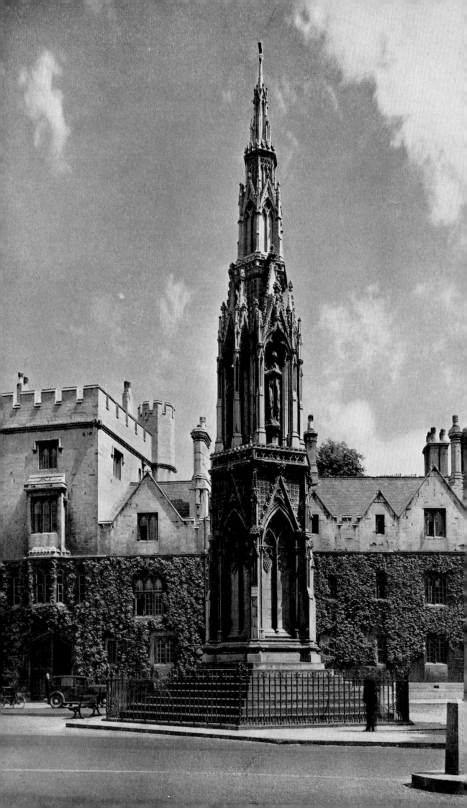

Nineteenth-Century Oxford
as it was

A NTHONY WOOD RECORDED IN 1669 THE START OF A SERVICE OF flying coaches, which were to travel, with luck and in summer only, from Oxford to London in one day. He left the tavern door against All Souls at six in the morning, " and at 7 the same night they were all set down in their inn in London."

In 1826 the Lord Mayor of London visited Oxford with his aldermen. He left the Mansion House at eight o'clock, and arrived at a quarter-past three after four changes of horses. Every ten years had knocked about a quarter of an hour off the journey. The Lord Mayor's return to London occupied three days, for he travelled in his state barge down the Thames, sleeping at Reading and Windsor. His chaplain wrote an account of the whole trip, which is perhaps the most sententious work of its size ever published.

So long as a day's journey lay between Oxford and the capital, the character of the former was not likely to suffer drastic change. Realising this fact, the university put up a strong opposition to the introduction of the railway. The first main line, projected in 1835, was not permitted, as a result of opposition in Parliament, to approach any nearer than Didcot. Not till ten years later was a branch line extended from Didcot to Oxford ; and to this day the city occupies a very anomalous position on the railway map and in the time-table, for a place of its importance.

The coming of the railway did in fact coincide with the beginning of great changes in Oxford. In 1850 a Royal Commission was appointed to examine the state of both Oxford and Cambridge. Such an interference would have been inconceivable at the begin-ning of the century. It was to be but the first of several such inquiries, Acts of Parliament, and other indignities.

" Pre-Commission Oxford " was a community in which Anthony Wood or Thomas Hearne would have been perfectly at home. Cobbett on his Rural Rides was moved to wrath by its smug apathy. " Upon beholding the masses of buildings at Oxford,

87 (*opposite*) : The Martyrs' Memorial

devoted to what they call '_learning_,' I could not help reflecting on the drones that they contain and the wasps they send forth. . . . As I looked up at what they call _University Hall_, I could not help reflecting that what I had written, ever since I left Kensington on the 29th October, would produce more effect, and do more good in the world, than all that had, for a hundred years, been written by all the members of this University, who devour, perhaps, not less than a _million pounds a year_, arising from property, completely at the disposal of the 'Great Council of the Nation'; and I could not help exclaiming to myself: 'Stand forth, ye bewigged, ye gloriously feeding Doctors ! Stand forth, ye _rich_ of that Church whose _poor_ have had given them a _hundred thousand pounds a year_, not out of your riches, but out of the _taxes_, raised, in part, from the _salt_ of the labouring man ! Stand forth and face me, who have, from the pen of my leisure hours, sent, amongst your flocks, a hundred thousand sermons in ten months ! More than you have all done for the last half century !' I exclaimed in vain. I dare say (for it was at peep of day) that not a man of them had yet endeavoured to unclose his eyes."

Cobbett ranted as the spokesman of the labouring man. John Bright more neatly voiced the disdain of the middle classes when he called Oxford "the home of dead languages and undying prejudices."

Hearne and à Wood might have found the same ample scope for their censorious talents in the habits of the early 1800's. "Drinking," we learn yet again, "is the chief vice of the dons. In a College not a hundred miles from the Radcliffe, is a tutor—a clergyman, of course—and overseer of the youth of his house, who had two attacks of delirium tremens in my time. In another College, hard by the last, the Head himself is constantly put to bed by his servant." The curse of coffee-drinking was still a fruitful theme for complaint. A new and horrid indulgence was the smoking of cigars. Even the senior members were known to fall into this habit, though in the presence of an undergraduate they would hastily conceal the degenerate weed.

Dr. Buckland, the Professor of Geology, was a typical eccentric of the day. His methods of research were all his own. Jackals, monkeys, and bears inhabited his house in Tom Quad. He claimed to have eaten his way through the whole animal creation, and the most curious dishes were served to his guests—"horseflesh I remember more than once, crocodile another day, mice baked in batter on a third." He stated that a mole was the worst thing he had eaten. On one occasion he was visiting at Nuneham, and was shown a precious family relic, the heart of one of the kings of France. "I have eaten strange things," said Dr. Buckland, "but I have never eaten the heart of a king before"; and down it went. Dr. Buckland "endeavoured to show that the whole of the enormous superficial deposits of the globe are to be accounted for by Noah's flood." He was no Newton; as Dr. Shuttleworth expressed it :

> " Some doubts were once expressed about the flood ;
> Buckland arose, and all was clear as mud."

With all their oddities and vices, these eighteenth-century relics, secure and celibate, moved in a singularly gracious world. Their manners were ceremonious. They wore their academic robes in the street, and no man dined in hall except in a frock coat. The Principal of Brasenose, then a foremost college, always took on extra horses for the last stage into Oxford " lest it should be said that the first Tutor of the first College of the first University of the world entered it with a pair."

The beauty of the coaching days was equal to their discomfort. " It is said in those days that the approach to Oxford by the Henley Road was the most beautiful in the world. Soon after passing Littlemore you came in sight of, and did not lose again, the sweet city with its dreaming spires. . . . At once, without suburban interval you entered the finest quarter of the town, rolling under Magdalen Tower, and past the Magdalen elms, then in full unmutilated luxuriance, till the exquisite curves of the High Street opened on you, as you drew up at the Angel, or passed on to the Mitre and the Star. Along that road, or into Oxford by the St. Giles's entrance, lumbered at midnight Pickford's vast waggons with their six musically belled horses ; sped stage-coaches all day long—Tantivy, Defiance, Rival, Regulator, Mazeppa, Dart, Magnet, Blenheim, and some thirty more ; heaped high with ponderous luggage and with cloaked passengers, thickly hung at Christmas time with turkeys, with pheasants in October ; their guards picked buglers, sending before them as they passed Magdalen Bridge, the now forgotten strains of ' Brignall Banks,' ' The Troubadour,' ' I'd be a Butterfly,' ' The Maid of Llangollen ' or ' Begone Dull Care ' ; on the box their queer old purple-faced, many-caped drivers—Cheesman, Steevens, Fowles, Charles Horner, Jack Adams, and Black Will."

Nowhere do we see this twilit Oxford so well portrayed as in the exquisite water-colours of Rowlandson. Among glades of trees unlopped and in front of mellow colleges still unrestored, he paints the comings and goings of rotund doctors in flowing academicals, or the dalliance between young bucks of inhuman elegance and local beauties of robust development. Over all the paintings there broods a Thames-valley haze, a sense of timeless ease.

This old corrupt, self-satisfied Oxford, which had long since ceased to grow or to evolve, staged a dying triumph in the year 1814, when the Allied Sovereigns came to England in premature celebration of the downfall of Napoleon. The Prince Regent and

14   85

the Duke of York; the Tsar of Russia and the King of Prussia; Wellington, Blücher, and Metternich all came to Oxford on a jaunt. Degrees were conferred in the Sheldonian amid under-graduate uproar; banquets were partaken in the Radcliffe Camera and Christ Church Hall. The setting, the atmosphere was just as it might have been a century earlier; but beneath all the unaltered ritual a deep change was at work.

Wellington himself is perhaps the last representative of the old order. He became Chancellor a few years later, and held the office till his death. His last days on earth were spent in an en-deavour to master an immense Blue book produced by one of the Royal Commissions on the affairs of the university. Wellington was not an Oxford man. His Latin speeches were adorned with false quantities. Under the present system of examinations, it would have been impossible for this supreme soldier and diplomat ever to have entered the army or the civil service. It may be conceived that he was out of sympathy with the reforms of his day, for the chief of these was the introduction of the examination system.

Cyril Jackson, an assiduous Dean of Christ Church, was mainly responsible for the adoption of the Examination Statute of 1801. His still more assiduous pupil, Robert Peel, was the first man to achieve a " double first." Thus was a future Prime Minister to be identified by his ability to cram his adolescent brain with likely answers to likely questions. The merits of the new system were obvious; its disadvantages were less obvious. It was good enough for the type of nineteenth-century progressive to whom the obvious was all in all.

From Jackson's time onwards there has been a tendency to classify all graduates as " first-class men " or otherwise, according to their fortuitous performance before the examiners at an age when they may either be quite undeveloped or fully qualified or already stale. It was the " first-class men," the Peels and the Gladstones, who were chosen to represent the university in Par-liament; it was they who used that trust to knock away the legal props of the university and the established Church; it was they who sent Royal Commissions to superimpose their cocksure recommendations upon the development of centuries.

Oxford won back a brief renown by its own passionate resistance to the destructive activities of its own " first-class men." There was a great Provost of Oriel, Edward Copleston, who had no faith in what he called " the quackery of the schools." Oriel had lately initiated the revolutionary system of electing fellows from among the members of other colleges. Under the regime of Copleston, they were chosen for their intellects and not for their degrees. Keble came to Oriel from Corpus with a double first; Newman followed him from Trinity, having all but failed to obtain a degree

88   Eminent Victorians : Sir Henry Acland, Jowett
(*centre*), and Dr. Wood of Trinity

F. Willan, Ex. C., Bow.

A. S. Yarborow, Lin. C.

Jas. C. Tinne, Univ. C.

S. Darbishire, Ball. C.,
    Stroke.

F. H. Hall, Corp. C., Cox.

89   The Oxford Crew, 1869

90   Gentleman Commoner   91   Nobleman   92   Pro proctor

From *Ackermann's " Oxford "*

93   " Show Sunday in the Long Walk," from *Tom Brown at Oxford* (1861)

94 Scholar 95 Bachelor of Arts 96 Student in Civil Law

97 " A Wine "

98 " After a Breakfast." Both from *Tom Brown at Oxford*

99   Rooms in College in the 'Seventies

100   The High in the 'Seventies

at all. By the end of Copleston's period, the senior common room at Oriel was the admitted head and centre of the university.

Oriel College, founded by a Rector of St. Mary's, has always held the advowson of the University Church. Newman was chosen for this important living at the age of twenty-seven, and he held it from 1828 to 1843. During those fifteen years the pews, in which generations of doctors had dutifully nodded, were packed with eager and excited listeners. The art of preaching was reborn. Newman was the master of an exquisite English style; and his message was further adorned with a wonderful modulation of voice. "Through the silence of that high Gothic building," wrote one who heard him, "the words fell on the ear like the measured drippings of water in some vast dim cave."

The year 1833, which followed the Reform Bill, saw the initiation of many legislative schemes in which the spirit of Jeremy Bentham and Joseph Hume was more conspicuous than the inspiration of Christianity. In that year the pulpit of St. Mary's upon which Newman had cast such lustre was occupied for a day by his friend Keble, who was to preach the usual assize sermon before one of His Majesty's judges. He took as his subject " National Apostasy," by which he meant the growing disrespect of the legislature for the establishment, and the divorce which the State appeared to be seeking from its spouse the Church. His sermon was a defiant re-statement after two centuries of the views which had brought Archbishop Laud to glory and disaster.

Keble's sermon created a stir in other places than Oxford. The spirit of the reformed Parliament was evangelical, if not dissenting. The vogue was all for legislation of the most scientific and secular description. Chadwick and Exeter Hall were the apostle and the temple of the prevailing worship; Blue books were its gospels. The Church and its privileges were regarded rather as the Lord Mayor of London and his satellites are regarded to-day. And if there was one place more than another which symbolised the decay of the establishment, it was Oxford.

Now, after generations of slightly alcoholic slumber, the Church aroused itself, and at Oxford of all places, to claim its Elizabethan status as an equal partner with the State in the affairs of men. The Oriel group, led by Keble, Newman, and Pusey, took full advantage of the sensational effect of Keble's sermon by starting at once the issue of their *Tracts for the Times*. They aroused fierce controversy. They were bitterly attacked; most notably by Arnold of Rugby, another fellow of Oriel. They were accused of ritualism, of an insidious tendency towards Rome. But for a time it seemed as if they would succeed in the regeneration of the Church of England. They were not ritualists; their whole claim was that the English Church was one with the mediæval church whose shrines it had inherited.

The failure of the Oxford Movement showed that the English Church did not embrace this flattering pedigree. As a progenitor, it preferred Henry the Eighth to St. Peter. Newman, the leader of the movement, overstepped the mark with his ninetieth *Tract*, in which he sought to reconcile the Thirty-Nine Articles with Catholic doctrine. His tract was condemned in Convocation ; he resigned the vicarage of St. Mary's, and went into retirement. After two years of tormented indecision, he was received into the Catholic Church. His conversion gave an affirmative answer to all the angry and hostile questions which had been aroused by the activities of the movement. From that moment it was utterly dead ; its postulates were proved to be untenable by the action of its own leader. Among those who had fallen beneath Newman's spell there was a landslide of conversions. Keble retired to his Hampshire vicarage. The empty name of the movement only survived to give feeble impetus to an effeminate ritualism.

These controversies are being forgotten. Oxford no longer thunders with accusations and condemnations ; Erastians and Socinians no longer cut one another in the streets ; and the conversion to Rome of an occasional curate does not electrify the university. Pusey [1] is commemorated by an obscure institution in St. Giles's. Keble has given his name to a new college.

Amid this domestic storm of sermons, tracts, and conversions, Parliament proceeded to enforce its will upon the university. One by one the barriers so long manned against catholics and non-conformists were torn down. Royal Commissions presented revolutionary reports ; Convocation and Congregation retreated protesting before the force of national opinion. It seemed to the older members of the university that all their institutions would be swamped under the onrush of new sects and classes. Papists on one side and dissenters on the other were to invade the sacred territory of the established church. In one year, " non-collegiate students " were to be admitted ; next, the establishment of women's colleges was mooted. And when the fellows were allowed to marry, it seemed that change and decay could go no farther.

The alarmed conservatives had underestimated their own powers of resistance. The university was very rich and arrogant ; those who knocked at its gates were poor and shy. In fact, when the gates were opened, they were too shy to come inside. They camped outside the coveted city. The nonconformists had qualms lest the pure bigotry of their students should be corrupted ; so they sat themselves down in mournful seclusion in the vicinity

---

[1] " He was in the three-horse omnibus which used to run from Oxford to the railway at Steventon, and a garrulous lady talked to him of the Newmanites and of Dr. Pusey, adding that the latter, she was credibly informed, sacrificed a lamb every Friday. ' I thought I ought to tell her,' he said ; ' so I answered, " My dear Madam, I am Dr. Pusey, and I do not know how to kill a lamb." ' "

of the Parks. The staunch pioneers among the women remembered that there were dangers of another sort ; so they built themselves a chain of suburban fortresses, Bastilles of antiquated prejudice, at a safe distance from the infection of masculine ideas. Only the catholics discreetly installed themselves in quiet and advantageous positions, from which they exercise an unobtrusive but powerful influence upon the undergraduate body. The great waves of middle-class invasion have spent themselves : the citadel remains intact. All round the university has been established a medley of miscellaneous institutions for the instruction of this or that sect or class or sex or party. Within these institutions, the qualities of intolerance, prejudice, and exclusiveness thrive and pullulate. But inside the university and among the ancient colleges, they are extinct.

Nineteenth-Century Oxford
as it is

A TOUR OF NINETEENTH-CENTURY OXFORD HAS ITS PAINFUL moments; but it starts pleasantly enough in Beaumont Street, which leads down to the front of Worcester College, past the former grounds of Beaumont Palace.

Beaumont Street is Oxford's only specimen of the Regency style. Its pleasant curve, its harmonious lines of cornice and balcony, form a composition more characteristic of a once fashionable spa, such as Cheltenham or Tunbridge Wells. In a city so packed with architectural ostentation, this unassuming residential street is singularly charming, though its attraction is apparently lost upon the modernistic eye. It has miraculously survived the nineteenth century, unmarred by so much as a doorway out of keeping : may it have equal good fortune in the twentieth.

At the east end of Beaumont Street, facing the Randolph Hotel, stand the imposing buildings of the Ashmolean and Taylorian Institutes. This block, a perfect example of the short-lived Greek revival, was built in the 1840's by Samuel Pepys Cockerell, the most successful of the little group of architects who stood out against the Gothic revival.

The Taylorian, which occupies the wing facing St. Giles's, is an institute for the study of modern languages, which keeps a fine collection of books in a fine library. The rest of the building constitutes the Ashmolean Museum. This is the university's private collection of curiosities. It consists mainly of (a) the remains of Elias Ashmole's collection, transferred from the " Old Ashmolean " ; (b) the Arundel Marbles, a gallery-full of Greek and Roman sculpture bought on his travels by the " magnificent Earl of Arundel," and secured for the university by his friend John Evelyn ; (c) a quantity of pre-Raphaelite works, bequeathed by a deceased official of the University Press ; (d) Sir Flinders Petrie's collection of Egyptian antiquities ; (e) a vast collection of drawings and sketches, from Michelangelo downwards ; and (f) such objects as Guy Fawkes' lantern, Queen Anne's gloves, and a lock of

CHRIST CHURCH MEADOW.

The Meadow Keepers and Constables are hereby instructed to prevent the entrance into the Meadow of all beggars, all persons in ragged or very dirty clothes, persons of improper character or who are not decent in appearance and behaviour; and to prevent indecent, rude, or disorderly conduct of every description.

To allow no handcarts, wheelbarrows, bath-chairs or perambulators (unless they have previous permission from the Very Reverend the Dean); no hawkers or persons carrying parcels or bundles so as to obstruct the walks.

To prevent the flying of kites, throwing stones, throwing balls, bowling hoops, shooting arrows, firing guns or pistols, or playing games attended with danger or inconvenience to passers-by; also fishing in the waters, catching birds, or bird-nesting.

To prevent all persons cutting names on, breaking or injuring the seats, shrubs, plants, trees or turf.

To prevent the fastening of boats or rafts to the iron palisading or river wall, and to prevent encroachments of every kind by the river-side.

THE GATES WILL BE CLOSED

101   The proprieties are still preserved in Christ Church Meadow

102   St. John's : the Gate

Cobden's hair. One way and another, it is not easy to discern the purpose of this weird collection. Its contents are of no use for reference, like books in the Bodleian, or for adornment, like portraits in a college hall. The university is no better off for the possession of a quantity of statues and potsherds arranged in top-lit galleries : Egypt, Greece, and Rome are all the poorer for their removal. However, museums are the rage. Anyone who dislikes museums is a Philistine. So you will be expected to examine Oxford's mantelpiece array with suitable intelligence and awe.

The worst of these kleptomaniac institutions is that they never cease to grow. Once inside the walls, no museum piece is ever seen again by the world. The Ashmolean piles gallery upon dreary gallery. Already the Taylorian has added a wing on the St. Giles's front, of which the half-baked design is a poor tribute to the system of education by imitation. Now, not two years later, it is the turn of the Ashmolean to extend itself. This time it is proposed to tear down a group of the pleasant houses on the north side of Beaumont Street, in order to accommodate more pots and pans.

Some individuals cannot see beauty unless it is imprisoned in a glass case, labelled and (approximately) dated by bookish authority. To the collectors of Assyrian brooches and pins, the unpretentious charm of Beaumont Street is of no account ; it is not accepted or recognised ; it is uncatalogued ; there is no leading authority upon the subject. But there are others less expert and less blind. On the south side of Beaumont Street, facing the scene of the intended outrage, is a new theatre, the Playhouse, opened in 1938. Its façade has been so built as to preserve in all their innocence the quiet proportions of the street. The architect is Mr. Edward Maufe, to whom high credit is due for this civilised design.

Many people suppose that the Gothic revival started almost overnight ; that after a given date around the time of Queen Victoria's accession, the classical tradition abruptly expired. It will surprise them to discover that the Ashmolean was built *after* the Martyrs' Memorial, which stands nearby at the bifurcation of St. Giles's. This was erected in 1841, on the third centenary of the combustion of Latimer, Ridley, and Cranmer, which took place just round the corner of Balliol. It is a very early work of George Gilbert Scott, then only thirty years old, who was to lay such a heavy hand on Oxford in the next forty years. The intricate design of this memorial renders it a popular trial slope for the night-climbers who abound in Oxford.

The Rubicon is passed. The Gothic revival has begun, and its worst excesses are at hand. The back entrance of Balliol faces the Martyrs' Memorial.

Balliol is the third in antiquity of all Oxford's colleges. Wyclif was once its Master ; Duke Humphrey is thought to have been a student. Only one corner of the mediæval college now survives. The main entrance from Broad Street gives on to a diminutive front quadrangle. Here on the left is the ancient dining-hall, now used as a library : in front is a short range of mellow Gothic of the fifteenth century, the upper storey of which has always been a library. Formerly this range continued beyond the archway in the shape of a small chapel of unusual beauty. Its place is occupied by a Victorian chapel whose colours and proportions can only be described as obscene.

It is hard to say why the rage for improvement took so strong a hold upon Balliol in particular. It started when Augustus Welby Pugin made a plan for the rebuilding of the entire college in the mediæval style of which he was so great a master. This scheme fell through for the reason that Pugin was a Papist. At later dates the work of destruction was done piecemeal by various hands. The chapel with its priapic bell-tower in the neo-Lombardic Gothic style was built " at enormous cost " by Henry Butterfield in 1857. It is a building so violently offensive to all the senses that half a century later its demolition was seriously discussed. Though the exterior survives, the interior has lately been expurgated by the installation of slick classical woodwork, reminiscent of a company board room.

The greater part of Balliol's front to Broad Street, including the main gate and the east side of the first quad, was built by Alfred Waterhouse in 1867-9. It is a clumsy and grotesque heap of staircases, but is without the actively poisonous character of Butterfield's work.

Two archways give access to the Garden quadrangle, a great straggling area adorned by some noble trees. In a corner of this quadrangle, adjoining the Master's house, are two pleasant classical blocks. That on the south side is by Henry Keene, contemporary with his work at Worcester. Its neighbour, on the east, was added by Basevi as late as 1825. Next in this gallery of styles comes an insipid post-war block, with huge effeminate casements ; next some inoffensive Gothic as far as the back gate ; and next a jumble of less inoffensive Gothic, hidden behind which is an excellent single staircase built by E. P. Warren in 1907 to finish off the St. Giles's front. Lastly, there is the gigantic hall which lords it over the whole quadrangle. This was a further work of Waterhouse, dating from 1877. The ten years which had elapsed since the Broad Street elevations would seem to have mellowed him considerably. The hall is at least a virile and energetic work, though without the slightest merit in its proportions.

Balliol is a college of fame and character. Innumerable jokes are based upon the supposition that its undergraduates include an exceptionally high proportion of Indians, negroes and others of darker complexion than our own. There is not the slightest basis for this popular belief. What Balliol does contain is an inordinate number of Scotchmen. It was founded by the parents of a King of Scotland. In the seventeenth century one John Snell founded fourteen " Snell exhibitions " to enable students from Glasgow University to proceed to Oxford. A Court of Chancery decided for some reason that they must go to Balliol, and they have done so ever since. Adam Smith was a Snell exhibitioner, and there have been many others hardly less distinguished.

Not all of these Scotchmen are young when they arrive at Balliol. Few of them are enlivening company. They drag on into their thirties, continuing researches which Glasgow should have completed, pounding like bulls around the rugger field, soaking in a dreary and indigestible culture. Their accents win them instant respect from English intellectuals : yet their performances in the academic world are far from brilliant.

In spite of this dead weight of earnest Scots, Balliol gained for a time, in succession to Oriel, the intellectual leadership of Oxford. This was due mainly to the personality of Benjamin Jowett, who was Master from 1870 to 1893. No book of Victorian memoirs is complete without a few anecdotes concerning Jowett ; but nowadays they seem to have lost their savour. He was a crabbed and whimsical old man. Yet there is no doubt that he exercised an extraordinary influence. Not only did he raise his college to the first place, but he contrived to advise and direct the lives of his pupils after they had gone from Oxford. Asquith, Milner, Grey, Curzon, and Bishop Gore were some of the undergraduates of the Jowett regime. Success and leadership seemed to be theirs as of right.

This spell of brilliance is over, though the jealousy which it aroused still clings to the name of Balliol. The college has fallen back into its Scottish rut. A staunch old-fashioned socialism of the H. M. Hyndman type is now the hall-mark of the Balliol man.

John Balliol was flogged by a Bishop of Durham at his cathedral door : two Bishops of Durham founded the original Trinity College next door. To this day the wall between the two colleges is a veritable Hadrian's Wall. Though the President of Trinity no longer stones his neighbours' chapel, insults are nightly exchanged. On festive occasions, the men of Balliol gather on their lawn to sing weird and offensive incantations in disparagement of their rivals.[1]

Across the road from Balliol, occupying the corner of Broad Street and the Turl, stands Exeter College, another ancient

[1] Another curious instance of how hard tradition dies. The great Lord Bacon had a sister, Lady Periam, who presented a new building to Balliol. On its site there is now an underground lavatory. In Balliol language, to make use of this convenience is to " visit Lady Periam," though few know why.

foundation in Victorian disguise. Founded as early as 1314 by a Bishop of Exeter, it was established in its original buildings just inside the city's north wall, in which the " turl " was a minor gateway. It was as a college particularly set aside for students of the West Country, and had bred some of England's most notable Parliamentarians, including Eliot, Shaftesbury, and Maynard. Its buildings were of all ages, while the garden crept delightfully up to the walls of the Divinity School.

The transformation of Exeter began about 1834, when the whole front towards the Turl was rebuilt in the Gothic of that day. Twenty years later, Sir George Gilbert Scott arrived and took things in hand in a still more vigorous style. He built the depressing block around the corner overlooking Broad Street ; he built the library ; above all, he built the stupendous chapel. This enormous " Early Decorated " edifice, which dominates the whole of the first quadrangle, is said to be based upon the Sainte Chapelle in Paris. It takes the place of a seventeenth-century chapel of great charm, which was so well built that it had to be destroyed with gunpowder. Nothing can extenuate the building which Scott substituted. It is a sudden departure from the whole architectural tradition of the university. It is out of scale with the college and out of keeping with Oxford. The most ingenious apologist of the Gothic revival cannot explain away its monstrous lack of proportion and reticence.

Inside the chapel is a fine Burne-Jones tapestry, woven in William Morris's workshops, representing the Adoration of the Magi. Across the quadrangle, on its south side, is a pleasant Jacobean hall, much altered in its interior. The fellows' garden, which is private, affords an exquisite view of the Divinity School. Apart from these features, Exeter has few claims to attention.

William Morris and Burne-Jones were both undergraduates at Exeter at the same time ; and at Exeter was born the friendship which produced the Pre-Raphaelite brotherhood. In 1857, when they were twenty-three and twenty-four respectively, a curious piece of good fortune brought them in touch with the born leader of their movement. In that year Dante Gabriel Rossetti came to Oxford and visited the new hall of the Oxford Union Society. It was his suggestion that the hall should be adorned with mural paintings ; and the two eager undergraduates from Exeter rapturously volunteered to help. Their friend Swinburne, of Balliol, also made the acquaintance of the master at this time.

The Oxford Union, scene of these hopeful labours, stands not far from Exeter, down Ship Street, and hidden behind the other frontage of the Cornmarket. The Society was founded as a debating club in 1823. The original hall, which now contains the excellent Union Library, was begun just over thirty years later, the architect being Benjamin Woodward, of the Dublin firm of

Deane and Woodward. It is a strange, high-pitched, octagonal hall, the gallery of which, interrupted as it is by circular windows, Rossetti and his young friends set out with so much enthusiasm to adorn. They chose as their theme the Arthurian legend, though curiously it was two years before the "Morte d'Arthur" was published. Rossetti himself undertook the Vision of Sir Lancelot, but never finished it; Morris painted Tristram and Iseult; Burne-Jones, the death of Merlin. The admirable decorations of the roof itself are also the handiwork of Morris.

This labour of love was not even rewarded by success. The young enthusiasts painted upon a coat of whitewash over damp brickwork, and within six months the work began to fade. In a few years it was scarcely distinguishable; and so it remained until 1936, when the skilful brush of Professor Tristram was employed to revive it.

When the Union Library moved into Woodward's building, a new hall, in imitation of the old, was built by Waterhouse a few yards away. The other rooms are dreary club-rooms, redolent of linoleum and lincrusta; but they still contain a few excellent Morris wall-papers.

For another and far more important work by Benjamin Woodward, it is necessary to go farther afield, as far as the outskirts of the Parks, where stands the Oxford Museum. This institution was built in the 1850's for the study of natural history, and its originator, a Professor Acland, was the intimate friend of John Ruskin.[1] From the first moment in 1854, when Woodward's design was successful in a public competition, Ruskin took an active interest in its completion; and the Museum may be said to be the only building in England in which the principles enunciated in the *Seven Lamps* and the *Stones of Venice* found a chance of authoritative expression.

Ruskin wrote with resonant eloquence of the successful use of his favourite Gothic for a scientific building. "Here was this architecture which I had learned to know and love in pensive ruins, deserted by the hopes and efforts of men, or in dismantled fortress-fragments recording only their cruelty; here was this very architecture lending itself, as if created only for these, to the foremost activities of human discovery, and the tenderest functions of human mercy. No other architecture, I felt in an instant, could have thus adapted itself to a new and strange office. No fixed arrangements of frieze and pillar, nor accepted proportions of wall and roof, nor practised refinements of classical decoration, could

---

[1] Ruskin was still quite a young man, but his prestige and influence were enormous. He was an undergraduate at Christ Church from 1836 to 1842, and his mother came to live in Oxford with him. After 1870 he was Slade Professor of Fine Arts. His lectures were riotously successful—in contrast to his attempt to exalt the dignity of labour by digging up the village street at Hinksey.

have otherwise than absurdly and fantastically yielded its bed to the crucible, and its blast to the furnace ; but these old vaultings and strong buttresses—ready always to do service to man, whatever his bidding—to shake the waves of war back from his seats of rock, or prolong through faint twilights of sanctuary the sighs of his superstition—he had but to ask it of them, and they entered at once into the lowliest ministries of the arts of healing, and the sternest and clearest offices in the service of science."

It was characteristic of Ruskin's ideals that he should wish each column in the hall of the museum to be made of some distinct mineral, so as to illustrate the science of geology, while the carvings of each capital embodied a different botanical form. One column, however, which he erected with his own hands, required to be taken down and replaced by a more experienced artisan.

The workmen engaged on the building of the Museum found themselves the objects of unusual attention. They " began each day with simple prayers from willing hearts," while " various volumes " were placed in the mess-room for their benefit. Ruskin had faith in " the genius of the unassisted workman." His faith was to some extent justified. Woodward brought over from Ireland his own workmen, and one of them, named O'Shea, proved to be a singularly gifted sculptor. Too gifted, in fact, for the various committees and delegacies in charge of the work. O'Shea's vigorous and insubordinate fancy gave offence ; he was dismissed : but even after his dismissal he was found at work upon the main porch of the building, furiously carving—" Parrhots and Owls ! " as he explained, " Parrhots and Owls ! Members of Convocation ! " He was made to deface these figures. Shortly afterwards, the funds for the building of the Museum came to an end ; and the stonework where O'Shea had hacked it may be seen to this day, just as he left it.

The interior of the Museum is a forest of cast-iron ribs and columns ; it houses a ghoulish collection of skeletons and embryos [1] ; but the hall is worth entering for a glimpse of faded Ruskinian glories. Ruskin himself was not over-pleased by the result ; nobody else has ever liked it ; Lord Tennyson considered it " perfectly indecent." Even the happy notion of a chemical laboratory copied from the Abbots' Kitchen at Glastonbury fails to redeem the prickly and insipid design.

The Museum has spawned around itself a litter of newer institutions : the Pitt-Rivers Museum, an Observatory, an Electrical Laboratory, and so forth. Two members of this scientific colony

---

[1] The Museum contains one great rarity, the head and claw of a Dodo. This bird, formerly complete, formed part of Elias Ashmole's original bequest. Having deteriorated in condition, it was ordered to be burnt by the Vice-Chancellor in 1755 : but the present relics were saved.

have architectural merits. One is the School of Pathology in South Parks Road. The other is the new Radcliffe Science Library upon the corner, built in 1934 by Mr. Hubert Worthington of Manchester : this library now houses the scientific collections from the Bodleian and the Radcliffe Camera.

Opposite to the front of the Museum stands a vast block of intensely Ruskinian buildings from which John Ruskin himself used to avert his outraged glance each time he passed them. Long before the 'seventies, the author of the *Stones of Venice* had been disabused of his ideas about the application of Venetian Gothic to English needs. But by that time they had branded themselves upon the orthodox architectural mind. Butterfield's chapel at Balliol was an early essay, contemporary with the Museum itself. The same architect is found at work in the same style at Keble College, nearly twenty years later.

Keble is not strictly a college, being what is called a " new foundation." It adheres to the university, but does not belong. It was first opened in 1870 as a memorial to the life and work of John Keble, and as a shrine of " sober living and high culture of the mind." Built mostly at the expense of the great Bristol family of Gibbs, it provides a comparatively cheap and inflexibly Church-of-England education for a large number of pious young men. They live in corridors instead of staircases, as a token of simplicity. Their quadrangles, whose level is sunk so as to prevent riotous assembly, go by the names of Pusey and Liddon.

As an architectural specimen, Keble exhibits in its most striking form the godlike self-confidence of the Victorian architect. Butterfield had no qualms about building in brick, although every Oxford college before his own was entirely built in stone. He was not in the least afraid of that tremendous variegation of colour and material which he thought necessary to offset the English climate. Above all, he braved heroic proportions. His chapel triumphs by sheer boldness. Butterfield's choice of materials is unspeakable. His glass and mosaics, bricks and tiles, brasswork and paint, all stand out as glaring and vivid as the day they were new. But his scale is superb, and his proportions are manly. Inside or out, there is nothing timid or mean about Keble chapel. Butterfield, in other words, had become a true architect. Only a crank could like his work, but it is a mistake not to admire it.

No visitor who is genuinely interested in architecture should omit to visit Keble and the Oxford Museum. If his appetite for Victorian monuments is whetted by the experience, he has only to follow in a northerly direction up the Banbury or the Woodstock Road to find himself plunged into the territory known as North Oxford. This district is a " dormitory area," entirely covered with large and solid houses of Ruskinian Gothic, which sprang up all at once when the rule of celibacy for the fellows of colleges

was abolished. Nowadays, the senior members being less fecund
and less well-to-do, many of these houses are converted into
lodgings. North Oxford is also plentifully supplied with Victorian
places of worship. Those who have acquired the taste will find
a valuable guide to all these mysteries in *An Oxford University
Chest*, by John Betjeman.

Those, on the other hand, whose interests are more limited,
need go no farther afield than the Parks. It is worth while to
return by Mansfield Road; for in this desolate spot are established two colonies of those hopeful invaders who have failed so
entirely to take the university by storm. Mansfield " College "
transferred here from Birmingham in 1886; Manchester " College,"
from Manchester in 1889. One is Congregational, the other
Unitarian. Neither is connected with the university. Their
buildings, the work of Basil Champneys in one case, and of
the Manchester Worthingtons in the other, are in both cases
surprisingly good.

The Gothic revival disappears as suddenly as it began. The
figure of Sir Thomas Graham Jackson looms enormous on the
architectural horizon towards the close of the century. We have
seen his handiwork at Trinity, at B.N.C., and in countless minor
restorations and additions. He is perhaps best represented in
Oxford's last genuine college, which is Hertford College.

The line of Parks Road is continued down to St. Mary's by Cat
Street. In the nineteenth century the name of this thoroughfare
was altered to St. Catherine's Street; at present, the signs describe
it as " Catte Street "; but Cat Street it is and always was. Both
the corners at which New College Lane debouches into Cat Street,
opposite the Clarendon building, are occupied by Hertford College.
They are united by an unmistakably Jacksonian " bridge of
sighs."

The new college inherited an old tradition. Hart Hall was
established on the site by Elias of Hertford as early as 1284. For
more than four centuries it was an appendage to Exeter College,
until in 1740 an enterprising Principal succeeded in obtaining a
royal charter exalting it to the status of an independent college.
Unfortunately he could not obtain the necessary endowments.
In the 1760's Hertford was sufficiently distinguished for Lord
Holland to choose it for his brilliant son Charles James Fox. But
this brief splendour lasted scarcely more than half a century. By
the year 1805 all the students and all but two of the fellows had
disappeared. Another decade elapsed, and there remained but a
single fellow, who not unnaturally elected himself Principal. Even
this barren distinction did not last long, for in 1820 the greater
part of the building collapsed " with a great crash and a dense
cloud of dust." It was then discovered that the ruins had no
owner, since the corporative body had ceased to exist. They were

103   Keble Chapel

104   The University Museum

105   The Ashmolean

106   Beaumont Street

therefore made over by the university as a site to rehouse Magdalen Hall, an ancient offshoot of that college. The present front dates from 1822. Hertford's final re-emergence as a college was due to the generosity of a Mr. Baring, of the great family of bankers. It was established by an Act of Parliament in 1874 ; but most of the buildings belong to the turn of the century. They are not really worth description, for Jackson was an architectural scholar without insight. The curious octagon which serves as an entrance to the northern half of the buildings takes the place of an ancient octagonal chapel in the city wall, known as Our Lady of Smith Gate.

Before abandoning the subject of nineteenth-century architecture in Oxford, mention should be made of two non-collegiate buildings by Jackson and Champneys respectively, both built in the 1880's. Jackson's vast Examination Schools stand on the south side of the High Street, at the corner of Merton Street. Champney's Indian Institute stands next door to Hertford, where Holywell joins the Broad. Neither building has many admirers to-day ; and indeed, both Jackson and Champneys have been beaten at their own game by a Mr. Hare, the architect of the inimitable Town Hall in St. Aldate's.

Modern Oxford

A HUNDRED YEARS AGO THE COLLEGES AT OXFORD WERE everything; and the university was nothing much more than an occasional committee of the heads of colleges. To-day the position is reversed, as the result of successive interferences by Parliament. The colleges are looked upon as picturesque, but not very important entities; while all power and control is in the hands of the university. The once proud position of the head of a college is sadly dwindled; and anything up to a third of the income of each college is confiscated for the university's purposes.

True it is that there survives the curious system whereby the Vice-Chancellor, the acting head of the university, is appointed by annual rotation from among the heads of colleges. The proctors are also appointed from among their younger fellows by all the colleges in turn. But these offices are not what they used to be. Formerly the Vice-Chancellor was a dictator, and the proctors were the dreaded instruments of his discipline. Nowadays, all the work of the university is carried out by a hive of committees and "delegations." One unimportant busybody may sit on a dozen different committees, while his more useful colleague can scarcely find the time for one. An able Vice-Chancellor can exercise much influence, but he can get very little done against the drag of such a system. The proctors are reduced to trivial duties. They endeavour to enforce a complicated code of rules concerning the use of motor-cars, or the suppression of drunkenness, or the discouragement of political violence. It cannot be said that the disciplinary rules of the university are either intelligent in themselves or intelligently enforced. The proctors do succeed in keeping the streets of Oxford fairly clear of undesirables. They still patrol the city just as they did when it was a sleepy little market town; but their endeavours are practically hopeless in the setting of a large industrial centre. In theory, no undergraduate is allowed upon licensed premises; but it is possible to spend three years in residence, and fully a tithe of that time on licensed premises, without being made aware of the existence of this rule.

Of recent years the proctors have lost much of their dignity by

107 The High To-day

108, 109　Life in a Women's College

a series of ill-judged attempts to put a curb on undergraduate politics. Communism and Pacifism make a strong appeal to many undergraduates at about the age of twenty. These harmless devotees label themselves as " students," a word abhorrent to the older generation. They start " student groups " and " student movements." Unfortunately, by exploiting the morbid interest which the daily Press takes in all Oxford affairs, they find it all too easy to create " student demonstrations " by means of simple publicity stunts. When it comes to disturbing the annual Armistice Day services, these performances cease to be a joke. The proctors, as representatives of the senior members of the university, are expected to take measures to prevent the junior members from behaving like the " students " of Cairo or Calcutta ; but with their singular ignorance of the methods of the modern Press, they have been apt to flounder deeper and deeper into the very scandal they have sought to avert.

The statutes of the university now apply impartially to women as well as to men. There are some 750 women in Oxford altogether. They were admitted to the lectures of the university in the year 1880, to its examinations in 1884, and to degrees in 1920. There are now four women's colleges. Lady Margaret Hall was founded in 1878, Somerville College in 1879, St. Hugh's in 1886, and St. Hilda's in 1893. Though their numbers are so small, a casual visitor to Oxford might well gain the impression that the women form an actual majority. They are perpetually awheel. They bicycle in droves from lecture to lecture, capped and gowned, handle-bars laden with note-books, and note-books crammed with notes. Relatively few men go to lectures, the usefulness of which was superseded some while ago by the invention of the printing press. The women, docile and literal, continue to flock to every lecture with mediæval zeal, and record in an hour of longhand scribbling what could have been assimilated in ten minutes in an armchair. Earnestly they debate the merits of their teachers— the magnetism of X, the eloquence of Y, the spirituality of Z—as though these insignificant pedants were so many Abelards.

The assiduity of the women undergraduates is stupefying. After the long morning's round of lectures they swarm to the Bodleian. Radcliffe Square is dark with their bicycles. After dark, in their own college libraries or in their comfortless little college rooms, they huddle for hours on end, stooping and peering over standard text-books. They are tremendous sticklers for tradition and routine. Every rule and regulation of college or university is literally observed ; the prescribed books are read from cover to cover ; the stereotyped opinions are faithfully noted and dutifully believed.

The women undergraduates have a truly Teutonic respect for their own dons, who in their turn take full advantage of it.

Spinsters almost to a woman, the female dons present a terrifying caricature of the mediæval tutor. They estimate work by quantity rather than quality. The fact that there is very limited accommodation for the women at Oxford, and that many hundreds of aspirants are yearly turned away, constitutes in the hands of the female don a scourge with which to drive on her pupils to ever more exaggerated efforts. By nature as industrious as bees, the unhappy girls are perpetually goaded on to the inevitable breakdown. If one of them shows a desire to select or discriminate among her subjects, if she deviates by inches from the prescribed routine of study, there is always the dreaded reminder held over her that others are waiting to take her place. Short-cuts are not allowed ; originality is forbidden ; however wasteful or slow, the whole of the scheduled course must be covered. The results of this obsession are clearly seen in the examination class-lists. Many of the women suffer actual nervous breakdowns ; others become stupid and mechanical. The great majority end up as school-teachers.

The women dons devote much of their thoughts to the dangers of masculine society. They have elaborated a code of rules and restrictions concerning the social relations of the sexes, which are strictly enforced upon the women undergraduates, and wholly ignored by the men. In a community so small as Oxford, the mixing of the sexes cannot be made impossible : it can be and is made a tiresome bore. To take a girl to a dance is a tremendous business, requiring special permission ; but nothing is easier than to take her all day in a punt on the river.

In practice, but little danger lurks in the path of the " undergraduette." About half the men in Oxford are no more adventurous than new-born lambs ; the rest, if they adventure at all, look in other directions than St. Hilda's or St. Hugh's. Very few of the women take the least pains to be attractive or even mature. Fifty years have not mellowed them ; they still care nothing for appearance or comfort. They run no tailors' bills in the High Street, but deck themselves in hairy woollens and shapeless tweeds. Germer's luxurious hairdressing saloons are unknown to them ; their hair is braided into stringy buns. Their domestic background is equally repellent. Instead of a quiet pair of rooms, guarded by an impenetrable " oak," upon a secluded staircase, each girl has a minute green-and-yellow bed-sitter opening off an echoing shiny corridor. Instead of deep sofas and coal fires, they have convertible divans and gas stoves. Instead of claret and port, they drink cocoa and Kia-Ora. Instead of the lordly breakfasts and lunches which a man can command in his own rooms, they are fed on warm cutlets and gravy off cold plates at a long table decked with daffodils.

In this setting the mind of the Oxford woman grows narrower

112 (*overleaf*) : Present-day Oxford from the Air

110   Leaving a Lecture, Balliol

111   The Pursuit of Knowledge

113   Early Afternoon, Merton Lodge

114   Between Lectures, Blackwell's Bookshop

MODERN OXFORD

day by day. In a detective novel called *Gaudy Night*, Miss Dorothy Sayers has described to perfection the small and unwholesome atmosphere of a woman's college. If any parent can read that book and still wish to send his daughter to Oxford, he will deserve what he will get. But there exists another organisation, the Society of Oxford Home-Students, which offers an Oxford education without a college life. This society was started for the assistance of the poorest, who cannot afford the dues of a college. Its members live in lodgings or at their homes, and number about a quarter of the total of women undergraduates. It is quite arguable that they come off better than their wealthier rivals.

Barely fifty years ago there were few scholarships at Oxford, and those were for the most part " close " scholarships from a particular school to a particular college. To-day it is estimated that fifty-four per cent. of the undergraduates receive some form of assistance by way of a scholarship.

Cecil Rhodes began this wholesale endowment. His last will, made in 1899, devoted a part of his wealth to the strengthening of the British Empire and of Anglo-American friendship in the interests of perpetual peace. He provided 60 scholarships for the British Empire, and 96 for the United States. His scholars were not restricted to any individual college ; they were to be chosen for their physical vigour as well as for their intellectual powers. By a later codicil, Rhodes allotted 15 scholarships to Germany ; these were abolished in war-time, and only in part re-instituted since then. On the other hand, the Rhodes trustees have created a further 40 Empire scholarships, so as to redress the founder's somewhat lop-sided geographical conceptions.

The Rhodes scholarships have been of untold advantage to all parties. Oxford has been invigorated by the colossal heartiness of the unscholarly " scholars." Its fame and subtle influence have been spread the world over by their dispersal. In the year 1939 a young Canadian parson, educated at Christ Church on a Rhodes scholarship, returns to claim the richest of all Oxford's prizes, the Deanery of its cathedral and the headship of its greatest House.

Apart from the Rhodes scholars, most of Oxford's poorer undergraduates are assisted by public educational authorities out of the public funds. Their presence in great numbers has brought about a change in the attitude of every type of undergraduate towards the university. Oxford is now less regarded as an experience to which he is entitled as of right, so long as his family can find the money. Instead, it is a place to which hard work and good fortune have brought him. The three years' education is no longer regarded as a pleasing interlude between the discomforts of school and the difficulties of the world. Instead, it is a strenuous period

103

of self-improvement and self-justification. The State-aided undergraduate is apt to be very immature when he arrives. He does
not mix much outside a small circle. He works incessantly :
perhaps he will take part in the jejune debates of that seedy rump
which perpetuates the name of the Oxford Union. His means
are narrow, and his future struggle for subsistence casts a gloomy
shadow over his present independence. This anxiety, and the
strenuousness which it engenders, spread their infection even
among those who have neither past struggles to recall nor future
worries to confront.

When an undergraduate succumbs to this peculiarly morbid
state, his adolescent mind, so far from being enlarged, is apt to
be daily narrowed. He plays for safety. His inclination towards
pedantry hardens into bigotry. He gains information in the place
of understanding. His tendency towards liberalism is crushed
beneath the weight of catch-phrases and ready-made opinions.
He emerges into the world with the disenchantment of age added
to the immaturity of youth.

This frustration of the whole spirit of the university is actively
abetted by a certain class of don. In every generation the don
tends to retain, long after they have become obsolete, the dogmas
that were in fashion during his intellectual prime. In the small
world of Oxford, a man of fifty may wield influence and win
respect by the mere repetition of the phrases and theories which
gained him his fellowship in happier days. Teachers of this
description seize upon the dissatisfied undergraduate. His dis-
content, a by-product so full of possible values were it to remain
fluid and molten and red-hot, is canalised and cast into old-
fashioned moulds to form a dead weight of stereotyped opinion—
cold, hard, and rigid. Liberalism's loss is Leftism's gain. The
shelves of Oxford's bookshops are crowded with the works of
Mr. and Mrs. Webb and Mr. and Mrs. Cole ; while scarcely a
whisper is heard of the tremendous tides of thought and action
which rock this island.

Parochial as it is, Oxford's leftist tendency is greatly exaggerated
in the public mind. Even here, though slowly, change is felt and
fashions die. At the Union, a Conservative President succeeds a
Communist. There is a large and thriving Labour Club ; but
there is also a still larger Conservative Club, and a considerable
body of Liberals. The members of the two latter organisations
are poor and irregular attendants at their own meetings. They
are men with many other interests and activities ; they take their
politics rather for granted. By contrast, the Labour Club is
almost a religious body ; and its members are never happier than
when passing resolutions, appointing sub-committees, moving
amendments, distributing circulars, and writing letters to the
Press. Their devoted activities, added to those of the " student "

115   Dons on Duty

116   Bullers off Duty

117   In Balliol Library

118   Dinner at the George

119   A Scout

120   Dinner in Hall

121   The Union Committee of 1895 : Centre row : F. E. Smith (Lord Birkenhead
(second from left) ; Hilaire Belloc *(second from right)* ; J. A. Simon (Sir John Simon
(extreme right)

122   " The Education of Arthur by Merlin " : one of the Pre-
Raphaelite murals in the Union Library

bodies already mentioned, create a public noise and impression out of proportion to their numbers.

On one occasion, the leftists of Oxford made news which re-echoed all round the world, and caused an impression which is still far from being effaced. In February 1933, the Oxford Union passed by 275 votes to 153 a resolution that " This House will in no circumstances fight for its King and country." There was immense sensation at the time ; there was apoplexy in Cheltenham and Bournemouth, and whoops of joy in Berlin and Rome ; but it would be altogether wrong to attach any serious weight to the resolution. Quite a few of those who attend the Union debates are Hindus of the minor lawyer class, who deny allegiance to any king, and would be loth to fight for anything but a rich client. It is much more remarkable that on any single night 153 ordinary, independent undergraduates could have been got to endure the tedium of a Union debate in order to defend the good name of that moribund body. And at the date of this celebrated vote, Herr Hitler had been Chancellor of the German Reich for less than a fortnight.

One way and another, the left-wing bias in Oxford politics is far less important than it seems. Many parents, with Oxford traditions behind them, have hesitated to send their sons to what appears to be a mere factory for the mass-production of socialist dons. Others, quite inconsistently, lend ear to tall stories of extravagance and degeneracy, of night-clubs, racing cars, and midnight orgies. They may reassure themselves. Behind all the newspaper noise and fuss, Oxford retains most of its old virtues, with all its old vices. It is exactly the supreme virtue of Oxford that it gives free play for the vices to work themselves out. Among the more well-to-do undergraduates, the drinking is still heavy, the debts still mount, and the snobbery of the minor gentry grows rank. But if these practices are not indulged early at Oxford, they will be indulged later in London, or worse still, abroad. Anyone who visits Oxford on a Saturday night will find himself in a bedlam of ill manners and conceit. Drunken louts throw food about the restaurants and make shindies in the cinemas. Each despicable little clique finds some other to despise. When one compares the behaviour of a Frenchman of nineteen or twenty, one may despair of English education. Yet before long, all these stupidities will be over and forgotten. Undergraduate behaviour, if it were indulged in a grown-up world, would lose a man all his friends and maybe his career. At Oxford he may behave as badly as he pleases till he tires of it, and start afresh with no ill-feeling.

Much unwelcome publicity has come upon Oxford through the use of its name by the Buchmanite movement. The adopted title of the " Oxford Group " is avowedly disingenuous. " It was about time for another religious revival of sorts in Britain. The last had come from Wales. That the new one should emanate from Oxford was befitting. Oxford would contribute the dignity so essential to a revival of religion. There was only one institution in England more suitable as the starting-point when regarded as news, for Cambridge had never produced a real live revival. But mostly I thought of Oxford as the home of new religions." Even so, it was not until this " religious revival of sorts " had been under way for nearly ten years that " Frank," with his wonderful sense of news, looked to Oxford to " contribute the dignity so essential " yet so conspicuously wanting among the intrinsic virtues of the " new religion." Nobody need fear that in sending his son to Oxford he will expose him to this particular form of proselytism. Buchmanism makes little or no appeal inside Oxford itself. In these days, its affinity with National Socialism is far too obvious for the tastes of most undergraduates. In its organisation and publicity methods, in its attitude towards money matters, in its boycott of the poor, it is altogether too redolent of the Brown House. Oxford will have none of it. In a hostelry where all comers may drink freely of the most rare and precious vintages of religion, of Catholic burgundy and Laudian claret, there are few who call for Wincarnis.

That Oxford survives at all is the fault of the public schools. With few exceptions, they still send out their boys at nineteen as immature as they arrived at fourteen. For five years every English boy in the ordinary public school is brought up in a biblical fairyland, where everything is either black or white, and every question is a question of morals. Women, he is taught, alcohol, tobacco, and the *Daily Mirror* are Wrong ; football, early services, prizes, and *The Times* are Right. This, Dr. Arnold's perspective of life, it is Oxford's duty to unravel and rearrange. The undergraduate must learn from the beginning the social scale of values. First he must learn the meaning of a bore ; secondly, that alcohol can be a bore ; lastly, that sobriety can be a bigger bore than alcohol. He will then be fit to take his place as a member of society. It must be admitted that he takes a terrible time about it.

Max Beerbohm wisely remarked that Oxford's business was to put back all the nonsense that was knocked out of us at our public schools. Some schools, and Eton in particular, still encourage " nonsense " in the sense of individuality. They send their sons to Oxford in a state of comparative maturity. For them, if they are otherwise qualified to start life straight away, the years at Oxford are a waste of time. But they waste it very pleasantly. Their rather more civilised existence is hidden from the eyes of the casual visitor. They entertain in a quiet but far from stolid fashion ; the undergraduates give lunches in their own rooms, and the dons give dinners and—an enchanting Victorianism—

128 (*opposite*) : Detail of a College Barge

124   Activity on the River

126   A Trinity Doorway

125   Tea in a College Barge

127   The Banks of the Isis

breakfast-parties. They have their clubs, of which the Gridiron is the chief, where rolls of bread do not fly through the air, and belching is not thought a social accomplishment. They have two small political clubs, the Chatham and the Canning, at which the level of discussion is kept extremely high.

Oxford's small plutocracy centres round the Bullingdon club. This body is vaguely connected with fox-hunting, and conducts an annual point-to-point. Its members attend fabulous dinners in expensive coats of a special colour. They are mostly very rich and agreeable young men, though a faint air of Junkerism clings to them and their Bentleys and hunters and hard-boiled fiancées.

More Bohemian, but still very civilised, is the Oxford University Dramatic Society, always known as " The Ouds." This club is a great feeding-place, apart from its dramatic activities. The public performances, mostly Shakespearian, are extremely good, all things considered. To more select audiences an annual per-formance, called the " Smoker," is exhibited with much wit and more indecency. The O.U.D.S. is Oxford's hotbed of intrigue. Its members are ceaselessly scheming to get on the London stage, to get a play accepted, to get Mr. Korda down to dinner, to get a commission from the *Daily Express*, to get the editorship of the *Isis* or the *Cherwell*, those two very dreary undergraduate weeklies. The greatest of all O.U.D.S. intrigues gave birth to the O.U.B.F., or Oxford University Balloon Federation. This organisation, which lived for about a month, gave out that Miss Tallulah Bank-head would rise in a balloon from the Oxford gasworks, and that Mr. G. B. Shaw would attend a public lunch before the ceremony. The latter proved to be Mr. Glen Byam Shaw ; while Miss Bank-head confined herself to kissing the aeronaut. However, a large public paid to see the fun ; and the revenue from newsreels and newspaper articles paid the balloon-hire many times over.

Some conception of the variety of Oxford's clubs may be formed by looking in at the porter's lodge of any college and studying the notice-board. For every ten undergraduates, there must be at least one society of some kind or another. This boundless variety of interests is one of the fascinations of Oxford. A man who is bored by all of them would be bored by anything. Those who are best catered for are the musicians. There is always good music in Oxford. The tradition, which existed already when the first music-room in Europe was opened in Holywell Street, survives in all its strength. In empty chapels, the organ scholars enunciate their fugues ; and the world's most skilled performers fill the Sheldonian with their harmonies.

No account of Oxford activities could aim at being compre-hensive, since they themselves change and increase with every day and hour. In this account, particularly, no mention has been made of the innumerable bodies which exist to provide organised sport

128 (*opposite*) : Christ Church and its
Neighbours from the Air

for those who were not surfeited with it at their public schools. But enough has possibly been said to suggest that life of the modern undergraduate is less drastically changed than the setting in which he lives it. It may not long be so. Privileges are being taken away, and unpleasant changes are foreshadowed. But Oxford is still a place of boundless possibilities. One undergraduate may put nothing into it and draw nothing out. His neighbour can still put in a little and draw out a hundredfold. The experiment is still worth trying, so long as a little of Oxford's character survives.

129, 130, 131   Oxford Notices

132   Saunterers in the High

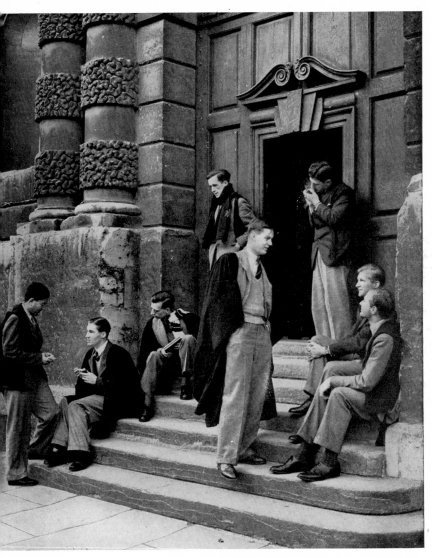

133   Outside Queen's Lodge

134 Rhodes House

135 The new Playhouse in Beaumont Street

Modern Oxford's Architecture

THE MODERN ADDITIONS TO OXFORD'S ARCHITECTURAL RICHES constitute a tale that is quickly told, and the quicker the better.

To begin in South Parks Road, the recent School of Pathology and the new Radcliffe Science Library have already been commended as seemly additions to the colony of scientific buildings. Opposite to them on the south side of the road, in what was a part of the Wadham garden, stands an extraordinary edifice, like a Cotswold manor house with a circular temple of heroic scale deposited in its forecourt. This is Rhodes House, built by Sir Herbert Baker, and opened in 1929. Sir Herbert Baker was a friend of Cecil Rhodes; but he has performed a curious job of work for the Rhodes Trustees. One wing of the buildings houses the Secretary to the Trustees; another contains the colonial and American sections of the Bodleian Library; the third consists of various halls and public rooms which are lent or hired for many purposes. What the rotunda is for, nobody seems to know, except that it effectually destroys the proportions and harmony of this costly building.[1]

Another knightly architect is as ill represented in the new block of the Bodleian, which has taken the place of a charming row of houses at the corner of Broad Street. Sir Giles Gilbert Scott, the grandson of Sir George, is an architect of undoubted powers; but in this work he has done himself something less than justice. He has banished proportion along with symmetry. The body of the building is huge and formless: its ground floor is ornamented like a draper's shop with a veneer of commercial classical stonework. From the librarian's point of view the design is said to be excellent; but this can hardly excuse its eccentricities of fenestration, or its insipid effort in the direction of modernity. Millions of little-used books are housed in this fortress; they are conveyed to the readers

[1] Sir Herbert Baker has perhaps subconsciously evoked the miraculous helmet which appeared in the courtyard of the Castle of Otranto.

by an endless belt or conveyor passing through a tunnel underneath the street. The total cost has been about a million pounds, of which more than half has been given by the Rockefeller Trust.

Cat Street gives its more genteel name to St. Catherine's Society, formerly housed in the Clarendon Buildings. This society embodies the male non-collegiate students, whose presence at Oxford was first tolerated by a statute of 1868. The idea of the innovation was to assist the poorest scholars ; but in fact the pull of the collegiate system is irresistible. Lodgings are expensive and often hateful, while private munificence is without end. Already St. Catherine's has a home of its own, though still non-residential. It is only a matter of time before it houses its pupils under one roof, and for exactly the same reasons which drove the mediæval scholars to lodge together. The present quarters of the society, built in 1936, stand at the bottom of St. Aldate's beyond the Broad Walk, on the site of a lately demolished slum. The architect is the ever reliable Mr. Hubert Worthington, who, unlike most of his contemporaries, builds for posterity. His work is solid enough to last, and its freedom from fashionable oddities will commend it to later generations long after tastes have changed. It may be noticed that the St. Catherine's building, in common with Rhodes House, possesses a Cotswold flavour which is new to Oxford. This is due less to design than to material. The old soft Headington stone of which Oxford was originally built has proved in the long run unsuitable ; and in many places it has had to be refaced. The hard rough Clipsham stone is taking its place. Butterfield's experiment in the use of brick has fortunately not gained ground except among the far-flung women's colleges.

Sir Edwin Lutyens, greatest and most erratic of living architects, is represented at Oxford by but a single work, the new Campion Hall which stands in Brewer Street, a few paces from the St. Catherine's Society. Campion Hall is a training college of the Society of Jesus. It honours the name of the great Jesuit martyr who was a fellow of St. John's College. Founded in 1897, it existed for many years in a large house in St. Giles's which was rented from St. John's ; but by an amazing feat of faith and will it has earned within forty years not only a home of its own, but a prominent part of the affairs of the university.

Sir Edwin Lutyens was given a narrow site in a narrow sidestreet. By skilful planning he has endowed his building with a serene dignity which is far beyond the reach of younger architects. The street frontage of Campion Hall is not wholly successful. It has an unusual feature in its red roof ; and the chapel is raised, by a masterly innovation, to the upper storey of the house. But, even allowing for the narrow area in which it can be viewed, this elevation is not wholly satisfying. From the little garden inside, the touch of the great architect can be seen more clearly. He has turned his little patch of ground into something tranquil and full of dignity ; while his interior is full of the riches of the incomparable Lutyens inventiveness.

Campion Hall, unlike the nonconformist " colleges," is a part of the university ; its scholars can matriculate and graduate. Under a recent statute, it ranks as a Permanent Private Hall. Two other bodies enjoy the same status. St. Benet's Hall belongs to the Benedictines, and is ruled by the Abbot of Ampleforth. St. Peter's Hall is evangelical. Neither has claims to architectural renown.

Mention has been made of the new Playhouse, designed by Edward Maufe. It was opened in 1938, and its graceful frontage upon Beaumont Street is a model of architectural good manners.

The various women's colleges lie far afield, and all except Somerville are built of brick. Though designed by a variety of eminent architects, none of them deserves particular attention ; nor does Sir Giles Gilbert Scott's new library in North Oxford for the Society of Oxford Home-Students. The abandonment by the women's colleges of the staircase system constitutes a fundamental departure from the Oxford plan, and any of their buildings might serve as a hospital or asylum in any provincial town. Balliol has lately built itself a block of cheap lodgings consisting of bedsitting rooms and corridors ; but it is unlikely that this hateful novelty will gain ground among the men.

The river is a last Oxford attraction. From Folly Bridge downwards for some distance its left bank is lined with ancient and elaborate barges, which serve as club rooms, dressing rooms, and grandstands to the various college rowing clubs. Many of these barges were formerly the state barges of the London City companies, and were bought about eighty years ago, when organised rowing began. Since then they have remained a picturesque feature of the riverside ; but they incur the displeasure of the serious rowing man, who considers that the river is too narrow, even without them. The Oxford boat races are limited to bumping races, and the team which competes against Cambridge has to go down to Henley for its practice. These barges with their rafts take up some thirty feet of water ; besides which, they are insanitary to a degree. But it is a pity that they have to go. Christ Church, which owns the river bank, has led the way by building the first boathouse—a design in hot red brick, by a former rowing blue. A row of these edifices will soon replace the cool willows : concrete ramps will oust the untidy grass banks. What matter if another mile an hour can be attained ?—but at least the Christ Church authorities might soften the blow by putting a coat of whitewash on their box of bricks.

Oxford and the Future

"THE PRIMACY OF OXFORD AND CAMBRIDGE AMONG THE ENGLISH national universities is, in my judgment, doomed ": so writes the late Master of University College. " The educational authority of Oxford will relatively decline. In another fifty years, or less, the most famous and influential of English universities will be London. This metropolitan drift is worldwide." If this prophecy comes true, it will be Oxford's own fault. Against the wealth and convenience of London, Oxford can match its splendid reputation and inheritance. It would be tragic if education also should yield to the vicious centripetal forces which are weakening the whole structure of England.

Already Oxford has surrendered much of its independence. The legislative interferences of the last century were accepted under protest; but after the war the university yielded to the lure of money what it had refused to the claims of " reform." A Treasury grant was the bait; and having swallowed it, the university has never since been truly its own master. It is now kept by Parliament to the tune of £110,000 a year.

While handing over its own autonomy to the State, the university has exacted from the colleges the surrender of their autonomy in turn. Though this development was well advanced before the war, it has now reached a point at which the colleges are mere vestigia ; and they will soon be reduced to the decorative impotence of city companies. This policy also originates in the university's insatiable demand for money. The colleges are now subjected to forced levies of some £75,000 a year for " university purposes."

Sustained by these two main sources of income, the university balances an annual budget of a little over £200,000. This vast sum of money, earned by such regrettable expedients, is laid out in grants to all those institutions which have least relation to the immemorial purposes of the university. The Ashmolean Museum has only to ask for an odd £20,000 and it is granted. A guarantee of £7,000 yearly, representing a capital sum of some £250,000, is allotted without hesitation towards the upkeep of the new

136   New College Hall

137   The Broad Walk in Christ Church Meadow

138   A Glimpse of Tom Quad

Bodleian, although the effect of it is to wipe out the entire surplus of the university's revenue. To maintain and enlarge these huge collections, which exist only for the specialist, in competition with governments, municipalities, and millionaires all over the world, the university lays its hands on ancient endowments set aside for the education of the young in separate colleges.

Greedy as it has recently been, the university has become rapacious in its demands since the advent of Lord Nuffield. William Morris, as he was born, was the son of an Oxfordshire farmer. One of his earliest ventures was a bicycle shop in Long Wall Street, which is still remembered by the more aged members of the University. He is now a Viscount, and one of the richest men in the world. His works at Cowley, just outside Oxford to the east, employ five thousand men; and the tradesmen of Oxford grow fat upon their wages.

Lord Nuffield is one of the few successful men who refuse to accept wealth as an end in itself. He has given millions away to his own workers, millions to the distressed areas. But he regards Oxford with a special fondness, as the city where his success was earned. He has given great endowments to Pembroke and Worcester among the poorer colleges, and to St. Peter's Hall. From the Trustees of Dr. Radcliffe he bought the Observatory and practically took over the Infirmary, in order to transform the whole site into a medical institute of the first rank. In 1936, he gave the sum of £1,250,000 for the express purpose of medical research. An immense school of medicine was to be originated, including four chairs for new professors. The university gasped at this magnificence. At a ceremonial meeting, held in order to express its gratitude to Lord Nuffield, he spontaneously added an odd £750,000 to his original donation. Later he sent £200,000 for the provision of new medical buildings, and another £300,000 for the improvement of hospital facilities.

These astonishing benefactions brought great publicity both upon Oxford and upon Lord Nuffield. The reaction of the university was characteristically inept. Its appetite whetted by these unexpected millions, it promptly issued an appeal to the public to subscribe yet another million pounds: the first £250,000 of this sum was to be earmarked for the purpose of carrying the guarantee so improvidently given to the Bodleian; the remainder (if there should be any) was to be spent on furthering the study of the Social Sciences, on the provision of modern science buildings, and on a variety of lesser objects, among which the extension of the Ashmolean figured once again. This appeal met with a very limited success. The general public proved unresponsive; but Lord Nuffield again behaved magnificently. He gave £100,000 to the appeal fund, and as much again towards a Physical Chemistry laboratory.

It will be seen that already in a few months the aims and purposes of the university had undergone a startling extension. Oxford was to become a medical centre comparable to Edinburgh, placed at the service of several of the adjoining counties.

In competition with Cambridge, it was to aim at the provision of the most up-to-date facilities for scientific research. And lastly, an altogether new ambition had arisen in the " study of the Social Sciences."

In the year 1935, the Rockefeller Trust made a small grant to the university for the vague and mysterious " Social Sciences." An Institute of Statistics was set up, various " research lecturers " were appointed, and the usual committees and subcommittees set to work in the usual way. It was apparently taken for granted that the scheme was to be for the exclusive benefit of the senior members of the university. " It has been suggested," wrote one of them, " that the grant might be used to help to form a bridge, both between theory and practice in each science, and between the different sciences ; to encourage the kind of research which is closely related to observable facts and can illumine the practical problems of administration and the current phenomena of our social and economic life ; to give a preference to co-ordinated and co-operative work, both between different specialists in one science and those in several which are brought into contact in specific practical problems. . . ." One can talk like this for ever without venturing upon a fact, or even a thought. One could read such a passage through and again, without ascertaining whether the sciences were to be learnt or taught, what they were, and why Oxford should be interested in them. Only one thing emerges—that among all this co-ordination, illumination, and bridge-formation, among all these problems, phenomena, and theories, the existence of the mere undergraduate has been overlooked.

If the university were honest with itself, it would call a halt to all this nonsense. It would remember the simple and pious objects of its ancient founders. It would reflect that never more than at the present time did England need a supply of young men fit to serve God in Church and State.

That Lord Nuffield should fall for the vogue of the Social Sciences was only to be expected. A man of simple tastes and upright views, he derives the wealth of Crœsus from an invention which is a curse to mankind. Between himself and those who take his wages is fixed a gulf which he would gladly bridge. He may well feel as keenly aware as any man in England of the ill-adjustment of present-day society. And it is natural that he should suppose that money, which can banish so much of disease, should be able to solve these problems also.

Lord Nuffield has given a million pounds for the foundation of a new college, to bear his name, and to be devoted to "post-graduate studies, especially but not exclusively in the field of social studies." The primary object is to establish a link between "the theoretical students of contemporary civilisation and the men responsible for carrying it on." In other words, a clique of brainy fellows is to be hired to think and think on behalf of those who act and make progress—sometimes too rapidly for their own peace of mind.

The university has been given this money to spend. In All Souls it already has one post-graduate college, packed with ability, unhampered by restrictions. One such college is enough. If the problems of contemporary civilisation were capable of solution on academic lines, All Souls would have solved them. It produces flowery words enough, and woolly abstractions in abundance. Nuffield College will produce more. Committees are conferring; Mr. Harold Butler, a Civil Servant, has been appointed Warden; the buildings are in the charge of Mr. Austen Harrison, the excellent architect formerly retained by the Palestine Government. The million will get spent all right; but not a single undergraduate will be benefited by it.[1]

"Nicholas Wadham, founder of Wadham Coll., Oxon., was wont often to say to one Mr. Orang a neighbour of his (who was accounted a wise discreet man in that country) that ' he had a good estate and had no children to leave it to, and his kindred to whom he thought to leave his estate did not care for him.' ' Why ' (said Mr. Orang) ' do as Sir Thomas Bodley hath lately done. As he hath built a library, so you build a college and you shall be remembered every day. It will last from generation to generation.' So Mr. Wadham proceeded and did all according to his counsel." That was a balanced age : after the library, the college. To-day the counsel would be different. Why, do as Mr. Rockefeller hath lately done. As he hath endowed an institute for social studies, so you endow another institute for social studies. In this way are the springs of youth and vitality dried up ; money is lavished upon researches and collections, while St. Edmund Hall still begs in vain for an endowment little greater than a professorial salary.

It is clear enough that, if this process is to continue, "the educational authority of Oxford will decline." Every year fresh thousands of young men are clamouring for truth and knowledge. When Oxford has spent all its energies on the establishment of institutes for vague research, and all its funds upon libraries and galleries and museums, the young will turn elsewhere for what they seek. Middle-aged parasites will oust the true teachers. Words and theories will take the place of knowledge.

---

[1] Nuffield College, incidentally, is to extend equal hospitality to graduates of both sexes. It will thus set Oxford yet another precedent, being co-institutional if not co-educational.

That day is not yet. In spite of modernistic jerry-building, the old foundations are sound, and the old walls will stand for many generations. For nearly a thousand years now, Oxford has by its quiet example taught dignity and the love of truth to the youth of England. There is still no place on earth where a young man will sooner acquire these virtues, or more lastingly embrace them.

Index

117